GARDEN GRACES

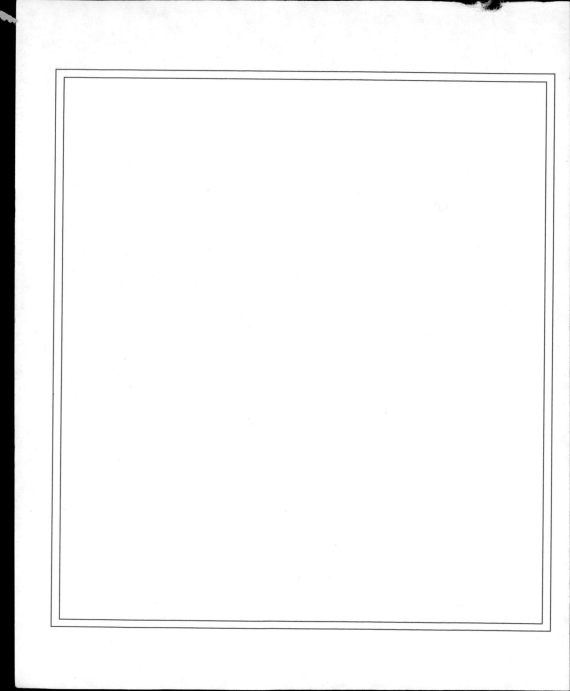

GARDEN GRACES

How the Simple Tasks of Gardening Have Affected the Art, Music, Literature, and Ideas of Western Civilization

GEORGE & KAREN GRANT

Cumberland House

NASHVILLE, TENNESSEE

Published by Cumberland House Publishing, Inc., 431 Harding Industrial Drive, Nashville, Tennessee 37211. www.cumberlandhouse.com

Scripture quotations are from THE NEW KING JAMES VERSION. Copyright © 1979, 1980, 1982, Thomas Nelson, Inc., Publishers.

Jacket design by Tonya Presley
Text design by Bruce Gore, Gore Studio, Inc.

Library of Congress Cataloging-in-Publication Data
Grant, George, 1954–
    Garden graces : how the simple tasks of gardening have affected the art, music, literature, and ideas of western civilization / George & Karen Grant.
        p. cm.
    ISBN 1-58182-059-3 (pbk. : alk. paper)
    1. Gardens. 2. Gardening. 3. Gardens—Quotations, maxims, etc. 4. Gardening—Quotations, maxims, etc. I. Grant, Karen B., 1955–   . II. Title.
    SB455 .G683 2001
    635—dc21

                                                    2001028077

Printed in the United States of America
1 2 3 4 5 6 7 8—06 0504 03 02 01

To Greg and Sophia
for all the seeds you've planted

The early morning is cool
And so sweet these days,
And the air is filled with birds singing;
The flutter of wings is everywhere.

The roses are pearled
With dew before breakfast
And the delicate gossamer of silver webs
Is spread out like a sheer sheet
On the deep, soft grass.

The rabbits have been about,
Nibbling tender garden shoots,
Or so the cockers say
As they tear out, nose down.

As we eat breakfast on the terrace
In the clear gold sun, the whole day
Spreads a breathless beauty before us.
The cats shake dew from their velvet-gloved paws.

The red and shell-pink ramblers are opening
Out on the white picket-fence,
And the Silver Moon is budding
In clusters of pearl.

It will be a busy day of ordinary living:
Peas to pick, borders to weed,
Kennels to scrub, cockers to brush,
And chicken to fry for supper.

There will be laundry to hang
Between times and tasks,
And a walk to the mailbox with Honey.
A wonderful day for garden graces.

GLADYS TABER, C. 1967

CONTENTS

ACKNOWLEDGMENTS

The satisfying labors of a gardener are among the most profound and paradoxical evidences of grace in all of life.
JOHN CALVIN (1509–1564)

It was William Blake who first asserted, "This life is no bed of roses." We beg to differ. Life offers us both fragrant beauty and thorny dangers. It offers fresh blooms and the promise of a thousand unopened buds as well as swarming pests and shriveled hips. It offers the dewy freshness of a spring morn and the bitter desolation of a wintry blast. Indeed, it seems to us that life is an awful lot like a bed of roses.

And we're not alone in that assessment. Across the ages, wise men and women have found a kind of universal revelation of life's profoundest truths in the doings of creation. Gardens have always therefore been, for them, laboratories of grace.

Thankfully, we have been blessed to know many such wise souls.

Jody Clark and Cindy Shapton are veteran gardeners who showed us the ropes, shared their secrets, traded caches of seeds, laid out new plantings, and grubbed about on hands and knees in our gardens. They did it all for the love of gardening—and of us.

Sally Bartels, though half a continent away, shared our zeal for hearth and home, for garden and grace. She has been an encouragement, a model, a mentor, and a friend.

Ron and Julia Pitkin are bibliophiles, not really gardeners—though they have always worked to ensure that their home is graced with beautiful landscaping. They saw immediately how our two loves—books and gardens—could be conjoined and offered enthusiastic support for this project from its earliest gestation through many missed deadlines. We are grateful for their abiding friendship, constant encouragement, inquisitive appetite, substantive interest, and unflinching vision for publishing excellence.

The soundtrack for this project was provided by the appropriately disparate music of Wes King, William Coulter, The Baltimore Consort, Michael Card, and Aoife Ni Fhearraigh. The midnight musings were provided by the equally diverse prose of Sir Walter Scott, Jan Karon, Hilaire Belloc, John Buchan, and Tim Powers.

To all these, we offer our sincerest thanks.

Of course, our deepest debt in life is owed to our three beloved children, Joel, Joanna, and Jesse. They have been our dearest, surest, and best companions in our garden and in our life. They are seeds sown upon fertile ground—and thus, they are the basis of our expectation of much fruit.

EPIPHANY 2001
King's Meadow

INTRODUCTION
It All Started in a Garden

The LORD God planted a garden eastward in Eden, and there He put the man whom He had formed. And out of the ground the LORD God made every tree grow that is pleasant to the sight and good for food. The tree of life was also in the midst of the garden, and the tree of the knowledge of good and evil. . . . Then the LORD God took the man and put him in the garden of Eden to tend and keep it.
GENESIS 2:8–9, 15

From the very beginning, mankind has been at home in a garden. In all the intervening years, we have found solace from the wearying effects of this poor fallen world among the flowers and herbs, trees and vines, vegetables and fruits—despite the intrusions of weeds, tares, and thorns.

Gardening has been rather artlessly defined as little more than growing and caring for plants as an enjoyable leisure activity, to produce food, or to create beautiful landscapes with pleasantly arranged flowers, shrubs, and trees. To be sure, for some, gardening is a form of exercise, a way to save money on food, or a way to ensure that fruits and vegetables are free from pesticides or other chemicals. But it has also always been more than that.

From Claude Monet's water lilies to Vita Sackville West's hedgerows, from Nebuchadnezzar's soaring hanging bazaar to Louis XIV's resplendent Palais Royale, from William Shakespeare's herbiaries to Hilaire Belloc's vineyards, gardens have shaped our world in often surprising ways. Not only do the images of the garden constantly recur in great art, music, literature, and ideas across the wide span of Western Christendom, gardens have provided some of the world's greatest thinkers, writers, artists, and leaders with the refuge and solace necessary to carry on yet another day.

Evidence of gardening dates back to at least 6000 B.C. Functional gardens have always been more abundant than merely decorative ones—people relied on their gardens not only for fruits and vegetables but also for plants used to make medicines and dyes. Elaborate, ornamental gardens were found only on the estates of the nobility, who had slaves or servants to tend the gardens. Thus, gardening for pleasure did not really become widespread until the development of the middle class, with the flowering of Western civilization during High Medievalism and the Reformation. With money and time to spare, many began to create gardens for enjoyment rather than simply out of necessity, foreshadowing the present-day popularity of gardening as a recreational activity.

But even when gardens were primarily functional, they were almost always beautiful too. The cultivation of flowers and herbs, fruits and vegetables, grains and tubers was always an inducement to creative and aesthetic expression.

Today gardening is practiced all over the world. Indeed, according to a recent *Wall Street Journal* survey, it is the most popular pastime in virtually every culture on every continent around the globe. With just a little soil, a handful of seeds, and a few basic tools, even inexperienced gardeners can enjoy the rewards of watching the miracle of life unfold.

Of course, gardening requires a good deal of work. And most of us do not much care for work. We complain about it. We chaff against it. We will do just about anything to get out of it. Nevertheless, we probably would all reluctantly admit that nearly everything in life worth anything at all demands of us a certain measure of labor and intensity. And though this might appear at first glance to be bad news—a plight of woe and hardship, perhaps a deleterious effect of the Fall—it is in fact a part of the glory of the human experience. It is actually good news that work is good. It is good news that the lost cause of diligent labor, strenuous industry, and purposeful calling may be reclaimed, restored, and reinstituted in the fallow fields of this poor fallen world—as the examples of so many wise men and women who have gone before have so ably and aptly demonstrated.

Thus, while we might be tempted to steer clear of the labor gardening seems to impose upon us, we nevertheless find in it a strange attraction.

Garden Graces is our attempt to explore this paradox and the resultant universal appeal of working the soil, husbanding the plants, and tending the harvest. By taking a long and lingering look at some of the world's most beautiful gardens and listening appreciatively to the legends, testimonies, quips, verses, and stories of the gardeners who created them, the mysterious joys of sowing and reaping become all too evident.

Garden Graces is thus as much an expression of our delight in exploring the effects that the simple tasks of gardening have had on art, music, literature, and ideas of Western civilization as it is our quiet meditation on the personal enrichment that inevitably comes to the backyard putterer.

Admittedly this kind of book bears the inevitable stamp of subjective experience. In fact, it is a companion volume to the Worldview Series, published by Cumberland House and designed to exposit some very personal perspectives of some very personal passions. *Letters Home* deals with the sage counsel of bygone days; *Best Friends* explores the ways friendships shape our lives; *Just Visiting* takes a look at the way travel has enlightened lives and viewpoints throughout history; *Lost Causes* discusses seemingly vanquished, yet always resolute, convictions; *Shelf Life* examines the bookish life and all its compliments; *Christmas Spirit* collects the joyous celebrations, stories, and traditions of the Yuletide season. Perhaps yet to come are additional volumes on sports, domesticity, music, handicrafts, architecture, food, and Eastertide.

The idea was to create a series of books that operated like happy conversations across the years and the miles—informed conversations about what a Christian worldview really entails in the most essential details of everyday life.

By its very nature, this book—like all the others in the series—is more a testimony than a documentary. These are our passions, our traditions, and our sundry favorites. Our purpose in writing then, is to both express and profess. And so we do.

The Kitchen Garden

*T*he kitchen garden is, of necessity, the most ancient form of the gardening arts. Indeed, Eden personified this type of garden in its beautiful combination of form and function. Typically, these seasonal gardens are not only reflective of the region and economy in which they are found, they also offer fascinating insights into the inhabitants of the homes they feed. This is why visitors may often observe painstaking archaeological digs into kitchen gardens of many historic residences—like that of George Washington at Mount Vernon. It is also therefore not surprising that poets and pundits through the ages have seen such gardens as perfect combinations of sheer pleasure and certain practicality—the quintessential vision of life at home.

God Almighty first planted a garden. And, indeed, it is the purest of human pleasures.

FRANCIS BACON (1561–1626)

I have always thought a kitchen garden a more pleasant sight than the finest orangery. I love to see everything in perfection, and am more pleased to survey my rows of coleworts and cabbages, with a thousand nameless pot herbs springing up in their full fragrancy and verdure, than to see the tender plants of foreign countries.

JOSEPH ADDISON (1672–1719)

A Garden is a lovesome thing,
God wot!
Rose plot,
Fringed pool,
Fern'd grot
The veriest school
Of peace; and yet the fool
Contends that God is not
Not God! In gardens! When the eve is cool?
Nay, but I have a sign;
'Tis a very sure God walks in mine.

THOMAS EDWARD BROWN (1830–1897)

Join this battle for Victory. Make your backyard a battleground for food by planting Ferry's Seeds.

ᴐᶩ FERRY'S SEED ADVERTISEMENT, C. 1944 ᶩᴑ

The size of the kitchen-garden must depend on the demands upon it, and the mode of culture adopted. It is bad policy to have it too large. It should be kept in the highest state of cultivation, and its productive powers stimulated to the utmost by liberal dressings of manure. The soil should be trenched at least four feet deep, and drained a foot deeper. All the coarse vegetables, such as Jerusalem and globe artichokes, horseradish, rhubarb, etc., should be grown outside the garden walls, if possible, in a slip by themselves. Herbs should have a border devoted to them, and be grown in beds three feet wide. Thus cultivated, the back-garden becomes a source of interest and an object of beauty.

ᴐᶩ *MRS. BEETON'S GARDENING BOOK,* C. 1883 ᶩᴑ

When I go in my garden with a spade and dig a bed, I feel such an exhilaration and health that I discover that I have been defrauding myself all this time in letting others do for me what I should have done with my own hands.

ᴐᶩ RALPH WALDO EMERSON (1803–1882) ᶩᴑ

Beneath the fruit tree boughs that shed
Their snow white blossoms on my head,
With brightest sunshine round me spread
Of spring's unclouded weather,
In this sequestered nook how sweet
To sit upon my orchard seat!
And birds and flowers once more to greet,
My last year's friends together.

    WILLIAM WORDSWORTH (1770–1850)

Now I am in the garden at the back, a very preserve of butterflies, as
I remember it, with a high fence and a gate and paddock; where the
fruit clusters on the trees, riper and richer than fruits have ever been
since, in any other garden, and where my mother gathers some in a
basket, while I stand by, bolting furtive gooseberries, and trying to
look unmoved.

   CHARLES DICKENS (1812–1870)

The garden is the interface between the house and the rest of civilization.

   GEOFFREY CHARLESWORTH, C. 1994

For him, work is vegetables. Most Saturday mornings, he is at his
stand in the Apt market, where he sells his produce. All of it is raised
à la façon biologique—that is, without the dubious benefits of chemicals: no pesticides, no weedkillers, no cocktails of growth stimulants,
no tweaking of nature. When I told Jean-Luc I had seen a shop in
California—I think it was called a vegetable boutique—selling tomatoes that were square, for easier storage in the refrigerator, he was
silent. His expression said everything that was necessary. He has
been growing his own vegetables naturally for years, long before
nature became fashionable. Enthusiastic articles about the return to
the earth tend to irritate him. Serious gardeners, he says, never left
the earth. But the revival of interest in organically grown food has
made him something of a vegetable guru in France. He is the author
of an elegant little book about onions and garlic—the first good
book I've seen that includes tips on how to repel vampire bats—and
has just finished another on tomatoes. Now he finds himself being
called in to create potagers for others. He will design your kitchen
garden, stock it, and tell you how to make it flourish. If you ask him
nicely, he might even come and eat some of it with you.

ભ PETER MAYLE, C. 1999 ભ

If you wish to be happy for an hour, drink;
If you wish to be happy for a day, cook;
If you wish to be happy for a week, sail;
If you wish to be happy for a month, love;
If you wish to be happy for a year, marry;
If you wish to be happy for a decade, read;
If you wish to be happy forever, pray;
But, if you wish to be happy all the while, garden.

ᴖ IRISH PROVERB ꙮ

A house though otherwise beautiful, yet if it hath no garden belonging to it, is more like a prison than a house.

ᴖ WILLIAM COLES (1626–1690) ꙮ

In the ensuing war years American benefactors were to contribute seeds to many British gardeners. By January 1943 ninety tons of American seeds were being distributed among members of the National Allotment Society. Their delivery was financed by the British War Relief Society of America. The seeds came in boxes which held seventeen or eighteen different varieties. Each box bore the name and address of the American donor. And a lot of pen pals were made when British gardeners wrote their thanks. Gifts of seeds also came from Canada, Australia, and New Zealand.

ᴖ JENNIFER DAVIES, C. 1989 ꙮ

If well managed, nothing is more beautiful than the kitchen garden:
the earliest blossoms come there: we shall in vain seek for flowering
shrubs to equal the peaches, nectarines, apricots, and plums.

WILLIAM COBBETT (1763–1835)

Morning has broken   Like the first morning,
Blackbird has spoken   Like the first bird.
Praise for the singing!   Praise for the morning!
Praise for them, springing   Fresh from the Word!

Sweet the rain's new fall   Sunlit from heaven,
Like the first dewfall   On the first grass.
Praise for the sweetness   Of the wet garden,
Sprung in completeness   Where His feet pass.

Mine is the sunlight!   Mine is the morning
Born of the one light   Eden saw play!
Praise with elation,   Praise every morning,
God's recreation   Of the new day!

ELEANOR FARJEON, C. 1931

Looking back, I realize it was William Lawson who inspired me to change our vegetable patch from its utilitarian rows of carrots, cabbages, Brussels sprouts, potatoes and leeks into a decorative potager, where, in his words "comely borders with herbs" and "abundance of roses and lavender would yield much profit and comfort to the senses." In monastic gardens up to Tudor times, plants were grown in ordered and patterned beds, with flowers specially chosen to decorate the church on Sundays and feast days. Herbs were used for scents and remedies and vegetables were produced for the refectory. Such were the kitchen gardens of old.

❧ ROSEMARY VEREY, C. 1994 ❧

Oh, the troubles we had that first year! No sooner had our vegetables broken ground than the deer started coming in at night and eating the plants. We decided at once that we had to fence the garden, but it was going to take a little time to get the fencing material in from the outside. In the meantime something had to be done. For a while we worked days cutting and setting fence posts, and sat up nights with a shotgun. But you can't keep that up forever. Then the game warden told us to spread some blood meal around. This is a packing house product that is used primarily for fertilizer. The smell of blood is supposed to frighten the deer away. It didn't, though. On the contrary, I think it attracted them. Then someone told us that if we made a little tent in the garden and kept a lighted lantern in it all night, the deer would keep their distance. The tent material had to be thin, so the light would glow through, and the color had to be changed often, so the deer wouldn't acquire the contempt bred by familiarity. We tried that—we'd have tried anything—and rather surprisingly it worked. At least, it worked for a week. Then one morning we went into the garden and found the tracks of a dozen deer, all converging on our little tent. Apparently they'd held a meeting and decided on a mass investigation. They hadn't touched any of the vegetables, though. I guess they were too intrigued with the light to bother about anything else. That very afternoon the wire for the fence came, and next morning we put it onto the posts we'd set so fast that it smoked. And that was that. That wasn't the woodchucks, though, that crawled through the mesh of the wire. We had to set traps for them. That wasn't the heavy rain, either, that gullied out the slope of the garden and washed out half the crop. We had to terrace the whole slope, the next year, to prevent a recurrence. But neither fence nor traps nor terracing was any answer to our basic problem. It's taken us all these years to lick its thinness and acidity and infertility. We've spaded in tons of manure which we've hauled from Miller's and various lumber camp stables, to add humus and give body to the soil. We've bought hundreds of pounds of lime and raked it in, to counteract the acidity which is always a characteristic of forest mold. We've scattered hundreds of pounds of commercial balanced fertilizers, too. What we've accomplished, really, is to make arable earth out of the rubble heaps of sand and clay and gravel that the great glaciers dumped here ages and ages ago. It may not be a becoming attitude, but all the same, we do point with pride to our vegetable garden. I consider that my skill with a spading fork is just as much a part of my housekeeping ability as is my urban sister's nose for a bargain in canned goods. They both result in putting better, cheaper vegetables on the family table.

❧ LOUISE DICKENSON RICH, C. 1942 ❧

Washington's Mount Vernon

The sucking sound of the horses' hooves as they laboriously pulled—*thwuck, thwuck*—from the mud only increased Martha's anxiety as the carriage drew closer to their destination. Home. How long had they been away this time? Seven months, at least. She peered out the carriage's open window, chin resting on her arm. Mud, everywhere. Was heaven itself conspiring against their longing to get back to Mount Vernon? The rainwater dripped off the roof of the carriage, finding its way onto her outstretched hand and sending a chill through her body.

After the well-intentioned sendoffs in the nation's capital, a flurry of papers dependent upon George's signature had arrived only hours before their planned departure. The farewell speeches, the lovely but time-consuming teas in Martha's honor, and all the delays in packing the household goods they would take back to Mount Vernon had left Martha bone weary. Then the rains had begun.

Friends tried to talk them out of leaving, but everything was already packed. Even George seemed reluctant to leave when he was presented with reports on the road conditions between New York and Mount Vernon. The desperate look in Martha's eyes had mirrored his own heart's desire, and they had departed for home. Plodding, that was the word for it. The final return of the war hero who couldn't be beaten by winter or the majestic British Empire was well nigh halted by water. Just too much of it. They should have arrived days before, but the trip had been slowed to a maddening pace. Now, they were almost home. Martha breathed deeply and attempted to sift through the damp mustiness of the interior of the carriage to catch a whiff of her own familiar fresh country air. That would warm her, even in this wet sloppiness of a ride home.

The sound of wheels upon stone woke her from her drowsy reverie as the carriage entered the drive leading up to the house. Home. She sat upright, pushing her hair neatly under her cap, smiled at George as he patted her hand and said, "Home." He looked years younger here, even as he returned the smile through deep wrinkles around his eyes and mouth. The carriage pulled to a stop just as the rain ceased. Sunlight broke through from low in the western sky, giving everything a golden-green cast. The couple stopped in their tracks and gazed not at their imposing, comfortable home, not at the welcoming staff arrayed busily before them, but at the entire landscape—the land, the people, and their beloved home all together. No one part could be separated from the other. The very mist rose up to greet them. Home. Early the next morning, Martha retraced her at-home routine, as if she had never left off. Walking purposefully to the kitchen garden, she held up her dress' train from the heavy dew on the grass. Had all the rain beaten every-thing into mush? Were the pea vines bent down to the ground? Were the seedlings drowned? Her brow furrowed, she easily outpaced the much younger kitchen maid, who struggled to keep up in surprise. There it was. Her own little domain of earthy domesticity, her own garden. Neat rows of emerging seedlings and early spring cruciferous vegetables greeted her. Not a weed in sight. George would be out fretting in his fields, overseers would be stuttering explanations, and fieldworkers would be rising from their morning stupor before Mr. President, who unfortunately for them knew better than they every inch of the land and the proper plan for its cultivation. She smiled at the thought of all the energetic goings-on in the fields today, and for the next few weeks, until George was satisfied that order was restored. He had refused the trappings of royalty as the nation's king and settled reluctantly for the title of President, but Martha was one of the few who really understood one of the most compelling reasons: this, Mount Vernon, was the only kingdom for which he ever had ambition.

She shook herself and turned to Betsy. "It looks very nice, Betsy. You and your helpers have done very, very well. Now, let's find a nice, plump cabbage to cook with the ham tonight. George will like that. He thinks it's food for a king." She bent over and squashed a cabbage bug between her fingers. If only gossipy Washington society had been so easily dispensed with.

What better place to observe a typical American garden than the home of our nation's father, George Washington? Although he served two terms as president, commanded the Continental army, and fashioned much of the nation's heritage, he considered himself, first and foremost, a farmer. This close association with the land—the valuing of its resources, the appreciation of its beauty, an understanding of its seasons—surely shaped Washington's commitment to public service as much as his understanding of the law and resistance to tyrannical rule. As one who loved and understood the land and its potential for productivity, he must have felt compelled to civil service as much for this sacred trust as by his love for American ideals. His very insistence of identity with the soil speaks much about his beliefs about the importance of agriculture to an emerging nation.

In *The Gardens and Grounds at Mount Vernon*, John A. Castellani relates that "Washington could little have suspected, as he looked forward to a gentleman's life on the banks of the Potomac, that of the forty years that remained until his death in 1799, the demands of the wide and bustling world would keep him away from Mount Vernon for nearly twenty. From 1775 to 1783, he led the Continental Army, paying only two visits to his home in almost nine years. Victory brought a brief retirement interrupted by the Constitutional Convention and, after that document was ratified, Washington left Mount Vernon again to be inaugurated first president of the United States in 1789. When he returned in 1797, he had less than three years to live."

Fortunately for us, the Mount Vernon Ladies Association acquired Mount Vernon in 1858 and began the painstaking process of restoring it to its height of glory. Visitors today reap the reward of the years of dedication of this society to preserving the home of Washington as well as his beloved gardens.

Although the plantation was a typical self-sufficient entity, with a vineyard; a greenhouse for more tender plants; nut, fruit, and ornamental trees; and vast fields of plantings for animal feed and products to be sold for income, it was the kitchen garden, or what was also known at Mount Vernon as the Lower Garden, that was most extraordinary. Indeed, it is the quintessential American garden: bountiful; beautifully laid out; filled with a variety of vegetables, fruits, and herbs; of a manageable size; and reflective of its owner's tastes. Set into a gently sloping hillside with a southern exposure, the garden has been restored as closely as possible to allusions found in Washington's letters and diaries.

The garden is maintained today to continue this tradition. It is rife with fruits and vegetables, a reminder to contemporary kitchen gardeners who often concentrate solely on vegetable production.

Washington's gardens contained several types of beans; root vegetables such as parsnips, potatoes, carrots, and turnips; lovely sweet green peas, a presidential favorite; tomatoes; cucumbers; and radishes. Fruits included apples, cherries, currants, grapes, pears, plums, quince, and several berries. Herbs were freely included, both for medicinal as well as culinary purposes. Basil, catnip, hyssop, lavender, lovage, nasturtiums, oregano, pennyroyal, rosemary, and rue are just a few of the herbs still found in the kitchen garden at Mount Vernon.

One of the most striking impressions we take away from this particular garden is how many varieties of fruits and vegetables can be grown in such a compact space. Hence, just as in Victorian gardens, most fruit was espaliered or efficiently used as boundaries between vegetable beds. While the first impression is one of the bounteous nature of the garden, a closer inspection creates a remarkable sensation of frugality and respect for land and labor. Thus, the design is one well worth close study even for today's gardener.

Beds are small and compact, with an obvious love for a variety of tastes represented. Artichokes are included with lima beans, and salsify along with lettuce. Ingredients for relishes and sauces are interplanted, such as horseradish, mint, ginger, and peppers.

To this day, a visit to Mount Vernon and her gardens provides a most excellent tutorial by Washington to the contemporary visitor. The kitchen garden at Mount Vernon continues one of the important legacies of Washington the Founding Father—the vitality of agriculture to a nation's economy.

An observant visit to any kitchen garden reveals that family's likes and dislikes at a glance. How many tomato plants? Are there any herbs nestled among the vegetables? Was room left for bramble fruits like luscious blackberries or red or golden raspberries? Are there several varieties of lettuce? Any peppers, garlic, or onions? Are the potatoes red, white, or blue? Is there a compost bin tucked away in a back corner?

A potager in southern France, for instance, might contain several types of beans, carrots, lettuces, tomatoes, melons, and berries varietal to the locality. Corn would rarely if ever be included, as it is considered useful for animal feed only. Herbs in remarkable diversity would surely be found, including rosemary, lavender, thyme, basil, fennel, savory, and tarragon. Garlic, shallots, and leeks continue to be de rigueur in the potager.

Kitchen gardens in regions of South America might be full of varieties of maize, sweet potatoes, cassava, yucca, garlic, chilies, squashes, tropical fruits, and grains.

Thanks to global television coverage, we are exposed to heartbreaking images of starving fellow humans, often in Africa. As the dark continent shapes and reshapes its political boundaries in painful emergence from both tribal and colonial systems, family kitchen gardens have increasingly become only a wistful memory. We wonder what enticing aromas are lodged in the memories of the human skeletons we see onscreen before us. In better times, for example, the typical Sudanese diet was full of vegetables as well as meat. Cabbages, onions, carrots, green beans, tomatoes, and okra would be a few of the vegetables grown in their kitchen gardens in better times, along with hot red peppers, dill, and garlic for seasoning.

In stark contrast, *The Victorian Kitchen Garden* by Jennifer Davies is a fascinating study of another place and time—the immense kitchen gardens that literally fueled the opulent lifestyles of ultra-wealthy landowners in Victorian England. Straddling the medieval serf system and the industrial revolution, manor holdings were in effect small townships, employing, feeding, and housing insular classes of workers in an intricate web of craftsmanship, industry, and dutiful purpose. Head Gardeners managed large staffs and followed careful regimens whereby large parties could be entertained for days or even weeks on end in regal country style. The Victorian glasshouse was essential, providing consistent heat and light for forcing vegetables out of season. Walled gardens with intricate methods of espaliers and trellising for fruit trees and berries made the most of available room and have provided tremendous bodies of knowledge from which the contemporary small garden holder can draw. Just as the American pioneer dug crude root cellars to store sustenance for the winter months, the Victorian manor house gardener was proficient at packing away soft fruits with leaves and packing paper in boxes kept in fruit houses to extend their supply. Root vegetables stored in sand provided an additional supply of fresh vegetables to the Victorian manor table, and opulent presentation of the food, called "dressing" the table, was almost as valued a skill for the Head Gardener as growing the food itself.

Kitchen gardens are still in transition even within our own hemisphere and closer to our own economic reality. During and after World War II for instance, the home garden regained vitality with the advent of Victory gardens. In our own country, these gardens served to free up food produced in commercial agricultural ventures for our own soldiers as well as to share with less fortunate allied nations whenever possible. The gardens themselves often served a second purpose: to disguise home bomb shelters.

During the war years, *The Home Garden Magazine* focused much of its energy on Victory gardens. Seed catalogs featured ready-made seed collections for victory gardens for every size of family. Kitchen gardening regained lost interest as it took a more serious turn for the duration of the war.

Simultaneously in Great Britain, the situation was much more drastic. Jennifer Davies' book *The Wartime Kitchen Garden, 1939–45*, relates just how vital home kitchen gardens became to the British war effort. The small island was able to stand alone regardless of the success of the Axis powers in forming effective blockades, which cut Britain's inhabitants off from fresh food supplies. Had the kitchen gardens kept up by the Women's Farm and Garden Association, the Women's Land Army, horticultural students, housewives, the elderly, and those deemed unfit for service not kept up a steady supply of produce, the courageous war effort would have crumbled.

Interestingly, as fertilizer became more and more scarce, composting methods were taught worldwide. Although many were skeptical of substituting compost for purchased fertilizer products, there was little choice but to learn to improve their soil in this time-honored method. Soil amendments from kitchen waste, animal manures, leaves, and other beneficial and free substances produced wonderful, if more labor-intensive, results.

Gardens themselves have even been targeted in wartime through the ages. A furious Samson tied flaming torches to the tails of foxes and set them upon the wheatfields of rival Philistia. Ancient warriors would salt the fields of conquered foes to prevent the economic recovery of enemies. German war planes dropped Colorado potato beetles on the Isle of Wight and in Kent during World War II.

In most of the modern Western world, we no longer face dire threats to mere survival. Why then, do we spend so much energy on foods that can easily be purchased at local farmers' markets or neighborhood supermarkets? Ask any kitchen gardener to describe the taste of a newly picked tomato or green pea, or to tell you about the race from the garden to the pot of boiling water with the season's first ears of corn. However, considering the lessons of Victory gardens in our own so recent past, one could argue that the culture of gardening is absolutely vital to pass on to future generations if any measure of self-sufficiency and even national security is to be sustained.

All said, the American kitchen garden may best illustrate

America's nickname as the world's melting pot. Typically, the gardens just outside the kitchen doors of many Americans include both vegetables reminiscent of our own cultural heritage and rare and new fruits and vegetables available to us at local home and garden stores or through one of the many seed catalogs. It's not unusual at all to find plump yellow corn alongside hot jalapeño peppers, Yukon Gold potatoes planted beside Blue Lake stringless green beans, Italian paste tomatoes interplanted with basil, lovely French Chanterais melon vines creeping past Appalachian moon and stars watermelon vines, and leeks and garlic reminiscent of the grumbling Israelite wanderers, all in a small kitchen garden in New Hampshire, Texas, or Tennessee. We are blessed!

For all the variety of seed selection, agricultural method, and cultural diversity, the overriding truth for any kitchen gardener is that the best taste produced is the taste of accomplishment. And since God walked in the Garden in the cool of the evening to enjoy His creation, so will we continue that most satisfying of occupations in our own satisfying imitations.

A Practicum on Tools

After gardening a few years with the cheapest and fewest possible tools, we began to realize that many of the things we read about garden tools were true:

- Buy the best tools you can afford so you don't have to keep replacing them. That doesn't mean you have to buy the most expensive tool, but don't buy plastic when you can buy steel. Check the way handles are attached to the tool. Flimsy tools are for indoor potted plants and non-serious gardeners.
- Take good care of your tools. Keep them clean. Put them away when you're finished with them. Keep them sharp. Many gardeners keep a bucket of sand laced with motor oil to store their tools, or at least to plunge them into once in a while. We think that's a great idea, and if someone remembers to buy sand sometime, we're going to do that too.
- Don't leave the rake or hoe facing up on the ground, or someone will step on it and get knocked in the head and/or cut themselves.
- Specialty tools exist because someone was smart enough to improve on a good design. If you don't believe that, go back to hoeing with a sharp stick. However, many tools are gadgets and gimmicks. You will also collect a few of these on your journey, but if you're careful, not many.
- Well-designed tools will save wear and tear on your back, your knees, and your hands. Therefore, well-designed tools are good for your marriage and close relationships.
- Everyone has a favorite garden tool. George's is an English edging tool, shaped like a half-moon, and he often edges beds

that already look fine just so he can use that tool. If he has a day to work in the garden, many things may go undone, but the edges of everything will be perfect. We purchased it from White Flower Farms in Connecticut, and he loves it. Karen's favorite tool is a Japanese weeder. It has a longish handle, is shaped like a triangle with one end larger than the other, and is sharp enough to uproot a stubborn dandelion before you can say taproot. It's so sharp that it comes with a protective leather sleeve. It leaves spades, trowels, and even those great "O" hoes in the dust. We purchased it from Smith and Hawken, on sale, which is just about the only way to purchase anything from Smith and Hawken.

- If people of varying heights will be working in the garden together, it's a good idea to buy shorter-handled or longer-handled varieties. It makes a difference.

Our List of Indispensable Tools

- A good digging shovel. This shovel should be fairly narrow, and long. It will save untold hours of digging holes for planting, digging up trees and shrubs, and replanting them. Our soil is rocky, with clay. Shovels matter to us.
- A good flat shovel. This shovel is necessary for spreading mulch and all the soil you will buy and compost you will make to add to your soil so that your hard work will pay off.

- A tiller. If you have a large garden, you want a large, heavy-duty tiller. We add so much compost, soil, and leaves that we are able to just use a small Mantis tiller. It's light, easy to carry, and works well inside our raised vegetable beds as well as the flower beds. We like it a lot, but we have found it difficult to start. We want to ask the people at Mantis why all their advertising shows women all dressed up to go out on the town while holding their tiller. No gardener we've ever seen dresses as they do when they're out tilling. If you have wonderful, friable soil, you may be able to get by with a cultivator. A cultivator is a round, toothed head mounted on a long handle that does a surprisingly good job of breaking up soil.
- A pitchfork. It helps in spreading mulch, compost, and leaves.
- A rake. Rakes are good for smoothing the soil just before you plant. Get a heavy-duty one. You can use the handle end of it to make grooves to plant seeds in, as well. Gathering up all the mess after a morning of weeding is made easier with a good rake. Oh, and rakes can be used for raking leaves, as well.
- Hand tools: the aforementioned Japanese weeder, a trowel, a heavy spade that won't bend in hard soil, and a bulb planter.
- Hedge clippers. Some people like electric. We have stuck with manual clippers and are satisfied, but probably don't clip as often as those with electrics.
- Hoses. Soaker hoses are great if you take the time to put on the

attachments and thread them throughout your garden. They really cut down on water usage and are most useful in July, August, and September, when it's so hot you kind of don't care if things die. Soaker hoses are already laid out, and you can run out in the heat, turn on the hose, and run back inside to have a glass of iced tea. You probably can't have enough water hoses. We have made some of our greatest mistakes here, buying cheap hoses that promise never to bend or knot up, only to find that they do so the first time we use them. Then we are stuck with them for years, unable to bear throwing them away until they get a hole in them. They are a miserable mistake. Watering should be a pleasant morning activity. Buy strong, durable hoses that won't kink up.

- Hose attachments. We like our watering wands. They are simply long extensions that screw onto the end of the hose and put out a spray instead of a gush of water. We think they do a better job of watering than a stream of spray. We also have a hose nozzle, which puts out a hard or soft stream. The hard stream is great for knocking off bugs before you make a concoction of two tablespoons of dish soap and two tablespoons of Tabasco mixed in a gallon of water—it is a wonderfully effective deterrent to most types of insects that will enable you to steer clear of harmful pesticides.

- Cutting tools. We like Felco pruners. There are probably other good pruners, but we like these best. We have three pairs, but try Felco #6 for small hands, #7 for larger hands. This matters in late winter and early spring when you are doing a lot of cutting back. Felcos are strong and will prune anything from a rosebush to small tree limbs. They are found in most garden catalogs and at good garden centers and nurseries.

- Scissors. We also love those large-handled Joyce Chen scissors. They are advertised as so sharp they will cut through a chicken bone, and we believe them. They are also small, so they are great for deadheading flowers. We keep a pair in the kitchen for kitchen jobs and flower arranging, and one with the garden tools for small pruning jobs, cutting twine, and deadheading. They seem to resist rust very well, also. Available in garden catalogs and at some garden centers. Don't buy cheap imitations that bend and get dull.
- Canvas carryalls. Karen keeps our hand tools, twine, seeds we're ready to plant, and trash bags in a canvas shopping bag easily carried around with us on gardening days. It has several pockets of varying sizes all around the outside of the bag that help organize our stuff so we can get down to business. We bought it for less than twenty dollars at the L.L.Bean outlet store in Freeport, Maine, and we use it every time we work in the garden.
- Buckets. George prefers the big five-gallon buckets and the

canvas tool bags that attach to them from the folks at Duluth Trading Company. They're called Bucket Bosses and they're extremely practical and durable. In the winter, they serve double duty as a ready-access toolbox—or you may just want to get several to serve all your utility needs. Of course, without the tool bags attached, the buckets are great for mixing soil, hauling water, scattering seeds, sifting rocks, or a thousand other practical chores.

The Public Garden

With the advent of the industrial revolution, the great cities of Europe and America began to transform themselves by punctuating their bustling urban landscapes with a network of public gardens, boulevards, promenades, and parks. The humanizing ideals of open public grandeur and radial, circumferential streets lined with trees became the hallmarks of cities like Washington, Paris, Vienna, and London. Extensive public park systems were developed in New York City, Boston, Philadelphia, San Francisco, Seattle, and San Diego. Pocket parks and neighborhood commons dotted towns, villages, and suburbs all across the world, creating some of the most intimate settings for the tasks of everyday life and providing some of the most memorable backdrops for art, music, poetry, and ideas in these modern times.

Everybody needs beauty as well as bread, places to play in and pray in, where Nature may heal and cheer and give strength to body and soul alike.

⊰ JOHN MUIR (1838–1914) ⊱

'Twas a park wherein all rainbowed flowers were heaped together, a refuge from the world yet strangely in the world.

⊰ CHARLES KINGSLEY (1819–1875) ⊱

Gently gripped by the
Avenues, left and right,
Led by the beckoning
Of some persistent wave,

You step all of a sudden
Into the meeting place
Of a shadowed water basin
And four stone benches;

In a separated time
That dwindles past alone.
On damp marble bases
Where nothing any longer stands.

⊰ RAINER WILKE (1883–1963) ⊱

God the first garden made, and the first city Cain.
                    ⊰ ABRAHAM COWLEY (1618–1667) ⊱

God made the garden, and man made the town.
                    ⊰ WILLIAM COWPER (1731–1800) ⊱

Anybody who wishes to study the unfolding of the landscape movement from its youth to its maturity, in its varying moods and with its
several motives, can find the essence in a single place by visiting
Stowe. Many of the greatest designers worked there—Vanbrugh,
Bridgeman, Kent, Gibbs and Capability Brown, each adding to the
work of his predecessors rather than destroying it. The early garden
of Bridgeman, formal but stretching open arms towards the pastoral
landscape beyond, with its buildings by Vanbrugh and Gibbs, was
the garden which Pope admired in 1731:
"Nature shall join you, time shall make it grow
A work to wonder at—perhaps a Stow."
                    ⊰ ANNE SCOTT-JAMES, C. 1992 ⊱

A public park is among the greatest gifts one generation can leave for the next. They remind us of where we have been and where we are going. They offer solace for the day, strength for the journey, and a healthy dose of reality for those peculiar moments when we forget that we are but mere men.

ꘐ THEODORE ROOSEVELT (1858–1919) ꘑ

A garden in the city ought to be the domain of the whole of the public. A tree planted in Boston or Brooklyn is a gift of solemn profundity—and ought not be proprietary. Public parks are the last remnants of true community in all too many of our bustling urban hives.

ꘐ HENRY CABOT LODGE (1850–1924) ꘑ

One wants to see one beautiful picture at a time, not a muddle of
means and material that properly sorted and disposed might com-
pose a dozen. I do not say that it is easy; on the contrary it wants a
good deal of the knowledge that only comes of many forms of study
and labor and effort. But the grand plants are now so numerous and
so easily accessible that we should consider all ways of using them
worthily. As far as I understand the needs of such a garden as I have
sketched, with a nucleus or backbone of pure formality, how grandly
one could use all the best plants. How, descending the slope, at every
fresh landing some new form of plant beauty would be displayed;
how, coming up from below, the ascent of, say, a hundred feet,
instead of being a toil would be a progress of pleasure, by the help of
the smooth flagged path and the wide flights of easy steps. . . . If
ground falls so rapidly that steps of such a gradient cannot be carried
straight up and down, we build a bold landing and carry the steps in
a double flight right and left, and then land again, and come down to
the next level with another flight. Then we find what a nice square
space is left below for a basin and a splash of water, or some hand-
some group of plants, or both, and that the whole scheme has gained
by the alteration in treatment that the form of the ground made
expedient. . . .

ⴲ GERTRUDE JEKYLL (1843–1932) ⴲ

In view of the work entailed and the cost, leveling should not be undertaken on anything but a very small scale, unless the scheme has been carefully considered and the site very thoroughly reconnoitered with reference to the probable effect on the drainage system. Where the surface is raised there will be little need for hesitation. Commence by staking out the area to be leveled, then select one corner as a starting-point, drive in a peg so that its head lies at the level to be worked to, and if the ground is undulating, from it dig trenches, the bottoms of which are all in the same horizontal plane. These trenches should radiate over the whole of the surface to be leveled and will show where soil must be cut away and where it should be added, also in what quantities. In these trenches start driving in pegs 6 to 9 feet apart, so that the heads of all of them are exactly level with the top of the first peg in the corner whence a start was made. Where a depression is to be filled in, or where the slope is even and not undulating, there is not need to dig these "trial" trenches, as the lie of the ground is obvious and the pegs can be put in at once, still working, of course, from one guiding peg. The earth should now be cut away from the higher parts and be transferred to the lower, being rammed hard down. The rough leveling completed, the garden-line should be tightly stretched from post to post—from the very tops, of course—and then the top-soil can be brought back and spread evenly over the surface and raked fine and leveled up to the level of the line between the pegs. The surface should then be rolled firm and should be left to settle and consolidate. When the soil has settled sufficiently, trial must be made that the level is true by means of the A level, any inequalities being rectified.

⊶ *WARD AND LOCK BOOK OF GARDENING*, C. 1940 ⊷

Using plants or objects to suggest to the eye a division, as well as using an actual physical barrier such as a wall, fence or the continuous planting of a hedge, is an effective way of establishing the architectural structure of a garden design. Upright shapes in lines or geometrical arrangements will emphasize a ground pattern and give a third dimension to the two-dimensional garden plan. As well as being architectural features, these divisions provide seclusion, shade and an opportunity to display plants in various different ways.

⊶ PENELOPE HOBHOUSE, C. 1987 ⊷

It is unchristian to hedge from the sight of others the beauties of nature which it has been our good fortune to create or secure.

⊶ FRANK J. SCOTT (1828–1919) ⊷

Consult the genius of the place, that paints as you plant, and as you work.

⊶ ALEXANDER POPE (1688–1744) ⊷

OLMSTED'S CAMDEN TOWN PARK

Growing up, both of our families moved around a good bit. Often, we would stay in hotels for weeks on end, until our furniture arrived and was settled into our new home. Sightseeing, dinners out, and card games soon lost their novelty. These were the weeks I read the works of Leon Uris, lots of James Michener, and smatterings of Tolstoy. In a new city with no sense of safety or bearings, getting any exercise and fresh air during this time proved to be a challenge, until I discovered great city parks. They were safe, at least during daylight hours, they were accessible by public transportation, and they were created for the pleasure of the public. Oases in the labyrinths of steel and concrete, they became a personal pleasure and outlet for energy. We love public parks.

Public parks exist for the pleasure of the city's inhabitants; they provide vital green spaces that aid in creating clean air, afford shelter and forage for wildlife, and furnish beautiful environments for exercise and play. World-class cities are known for their famous parks. Of even more interest, however, are small city parks—that pastoral acreage benefactors envisioned and worked hard to ensure would be located in the towns across America. These parks reflect the vision of some, the tastes of many, and, when well executed, the best in regional diversity.

Frederick Law Olmsted was arguably the most famous American

landscape architect. Born in Hartford, Connecticut, in 1822, Olmsted was brought up in a comfortable upper-middle-class family. His mother died when he was very young. He was educated by a series of tutors with whom he usually lived, until he was in effect inoculated against the very religion the poor country parsons who instructed him valued so highly. Academically, his salvation was an early and lifelong taste for reading. Spiritually, he found refreshment in hiking and appreciation of nature. Later in life he was caught up in a Congregationalist revival, but he never became a regular churchgoer.

Olmsted "tried on" several professions, among them business, seafaring, farming, and journalism. But, as is often the case, travel changed his life. Specifically, a trip to England exposed what would become his lifelong passion. In his delightful biography of Olmsted, *A Clearing in the Distance*, Witold Rybczynski writes, "England became the touchstone for Olmsted's ideas about rural scenery. He swallowed the English countryside whole, but he did more than merely succumb to its visual delights. His own modest efforts at landscaping Tosomock Farm had evidently awakened in him a desire to understand exactly how natural elements could be manipulated to create an effect of picturesqueness or sublimity."

After a visit to the park of Eaton Hall, Olmsted wrote an entry in his journal that conveyed his complete rapture: "A gentle undulating surface of close-cropped pasture land, reaching way off illimitably; very old, but not very large trees scattered singly and in groups—so far apart as to throw long unbroken shadows across broad openings of light, and leave the view in several directions unobstructed for a long distance. Herds of fallow—deer, fawns, cattle, sheep and lambs quietly feeding near us, and moving slowly in masses at a distance, a warm atmosphere, descending sun, and sublime shadows from fleecy clouds transiently darkening in succession, sunny surface, cool wood side, flocks and herds, and foliage."

According to Rybczynski, "The passage is striking for being as much an analysis as a description. It is as if he were compiling a checklist for future reference."

Olmsted eventually became an internationally recognized landscape architect, although he faded into obscurity soon after his death. His genius was in the wedding of his talents in city planning with an innate love of the countryside, which allowed him to create some of the most famous sites in the world. He died in 1903 in Waverly, Massachusetts.

His legacy was continued through the work of his son Rick, who carried out his father's dream to "make landscape architecture respected as an Art and a liberal profession." Rick was appointed by President Theodore Roosevelt to the Senate Park Commission, which replanned the city of Washington, D.C. He also helped found the National Park Service and became president of the American Society of Landscape Architects and the American Institute of Planners. The landscape architectural firm he founded continued in the footsteps of his famous father, whose sensibilities had been set in a childhood love for pastoral beauty.

Well-known parks overseen by either Frederick Law Olmsted, his firm, or his son's firms include Central and Morningside Parks in New York; Seaside Park in Bridgeport, Connecticut; and Battery Park in Charleston, South Carolina. His firm also developed the grounds for Stanford University in Palo Alto, California; Washington University in St. Louis; Smith College in Northampton, Massachusetts; Notre Dame University in South Bend, Indiana; Duke University in Durham, North Carolina; and Harvard Business School in Cambridge, Massachusetts. Rybczynski wrote that "between 1857 and 1950 the firm participated in some way in 5,500 projects." Olmsted literally changed the face of America, and all Americans owe him a debt of gratitude.

A fascinating pocket-sized park designed by the Olmsted firm can be found in the lovely seaside town of Camden, Maine, situated on Penobscot Bay. We traveled there on a day trip to visit the Farnsworth Museum in nearby Rockland, home of an extensive collection of works by N. C., Andrew, and Jamie Wyeth.

Way back in 1956, Louise Dickenson Rich, who knew just about everything there was to know about Maine, wrote of Camden in her book *The Coast of Maine*, "It would be impossible for me to say which of the towns along Penobscot Bay I like best, but I'd certainly hesitate a long time before passing by Camden. It's a perfectly lovely place. The location is naturally beautiful, on a high, wide tree-shaded bench of land with the blue, island-spangled waters of the bay spread out before it and the green Camden Hills rising abruptly behind. But a great many beautiful sites have been completely ruined by the hand of man. Such is not the case in Camden." We had no idea how picturesque the town would be, or how intrigued we would find ourselves with the town park, not to be confused with the 6,500-acre Camden State Park about a mile north on Route 1.

Camden Town Park is situated between the town's main street and the bay. On the gorgeous October New England day we visited, we found a little restaurant where we ate the quintessential clam chowder. Afterward, we were drawn to a community crafts fair across the way. As we meandered past the lovely watercolors, the inspiring photography, and the usual tie-dyed clothing and teddy bear trivia, we found ourselves standing above the blue water with screeching seabirds flying overhead. We squinted carefully off into the distance, hoping to be rewarded with a view of the puffins for which Monhegan Island is famous, but they were not to be seen that day. As we turned back to face town, we noticed from this perspective that the public library was located unobtrusively underground right before us, inhabiting a hillside in the park. It was lovely! It was the most perfect use of natural landscaping for a necessary public building we had ever seen. The small dimensions, true functionality, and beauty of the park were so outstanding that we wanted to know more about it. Consulting our guidebook, we found that the Frederick Law Olmsted firm had in fact designed the park.

It could seem to most uninformed home gardeners—including us—that anyone with a proper background in landscape architecture can design something magnificent, given the proportions of most city parks, plenty of money, workers, and locally outstanding natural resources. This fallacy is easily held until one runs across the tiniest of parks so well designed that the designer shouts—in this case from the ocean harbor on one side, the library on another, the town's main street from yet another angle—with sheer genius. The actual plantings in this environment are merely supporting actors in the celebration of the natural landscape. Synchronicity in land use and human structure can be found in famous urban spaces, but with proper principles, even in the tiny harbor town of Camden, Maine. We highly recommend waiting for a clear, crisp autumn day to visit. Plan ahead for the "form versus function" or "function follows form" debate. Camden, Maine, will provide plenty of fodder for either side. Just ask a puffin.

A Practicum on Visiting

Your best gardening moments are invariably in your own garden—certainly, ours have been. To smell the sweet pungency of freshly mown grass, freshly turned soil, and freshly harvested vegetables, to sit down upon the garden bench after a hard afternoon of labor with a tall glass of lemonade or a frothy mug of Saint Arnold's, to retire to the kitchen with a bucket of fresh herbs for an evening of gourmet experimentation: these are incomparable moments.

But visiting a wonderfully designed or sentimentally treasured garden in some far-flung corner of the world may come in a close second. Gardening is a communal, covenantal affair—one that connects us across the years and the miles.

According to the Latin proverb, "Travelers may change their climate but never their souls." While it may be admitted that this statement is essentially true, there can also be little doubt that travelers may at least change their thinking. Seeing the world—the different sights, sounds, textures, hues, and passions of cultures different from their own—affords them with a unique perspective that militates against prejudice, parochialism, and pettiness. As Mark Twain said, travel "broadens the mind and softens the heart." More often than not, travel serves to sunder our uninformed native preconceptions and to establish more mature perspectives.

For that reason, travel has always been part of a well-rounded education. The banal prejudice and narrow presumption that inevitably accompany an unexposed, inexperienced, and undiscerning existence can often be ameliorated only by the disclosure of the habits, lifestyles, rituals, celebrations, and aspirations of the peoples beyond the confines of our limited parochialism. The great Dutch patriot Groen van Prinsterer aptly commented to his students, "See the world and you'll see it altogether differently."

That is particularly true for gardeners. Some of our best ideas for our own gardens have come when we visited the gardens of others. We've had innumerable "aha" moments as we've walked through the gardens of favorite writers or the parks and pocket plantings of favorite cities. As Benjamin Franklin once quipped, travel can be "the laboratory where theory meets practice, where notion encounters application."

It should come as no surprise that some of the most famous books, some of the most influential perspectives, and some of the most remarkable social transformations have had their genesis in some great quest or expedition or journey or voyage—from Agamemnon in Troy and Caesar in Gaul to Marco Polo in China and Richard the Lionhearted in Outremer, from Christopher Columbus in the Caribbean and Cotton Mather in Massachusetts Bay to Charles Lindbergh in the *Spirit of St. Louis* and John Glenn in the shuttle *Discovery*. Just visiting has left an indelible mark upon the human experience.

When the Crusaders came back from their pilgrimages to the Holy Land, they brought with them a whole host of new ideas about almost every aspect of their lives—including their gardens. In the nineteenth century, when members of high-born families, aspiring artists, poets and historians, prospective members of the diplomatic corps, and young bon vivants returned from their obligatory Grand Tours, they not only brought back knowledge of the art, music, literature, architectural sites, historical monuments, social revelries, and culinary delights of the world, they brought back new notions about how man should relate to his natural aesthetic environment. Invariably, it changed the shape of the world. After all, as the contemporary poet Tristan Gylberd has asserted, "If you always go where you have always gone and always do what you have always done, you will always be what you have always been."

Now, whenever we travel anywhere—on a business trip, on a short family visit during the holidays, or on a vacation far afield—we always try to read up on any gardens we might be able to visit on the way or while we're there. We pay particular attention to civic botanical gardens, the historical homes of writers, artists, or statesmen, the big old city parks, and the restoration areas at the heart of urban areas.

Don't Miss Visits

Obviously, we would highly recommend a visit to any or all of the gardens profiled in this book—we've visited each of them and found inspiration, delight, refreshment, and encouragement there. In addition, though, we'd like to recommend some of our other favorite spots:

- **Central Park:** We love the hubbub of New York City. We love the frenetic pace, the wonderful restaurants, the amazing muse-

ums, the stunning architecture, the variety, the shopping, and
the theater. But most of all, we love the way Central Park
humanizes the city. We love the way it seems to be the heart and
soul of the city. We love the way it seems to keep the city and its
denizens sane, happy, and healthy. This vast public park is the
best possible argument for civic gardens.

- **Hever Castle:** Just around the corner from Winston
  Churchill's Chartwell is the storied castle of the Boleyns and
  Astors. But as wonderful as the castle is, the grounds are even
  more wonderful. The gardens are now open to the public and
  they are enough to transport every gardener to a kind of earthly
  Elysium. By all means, make this a must-see stop on any tour of
  England.

- **Sisinghurst and Abbotsford:** As long as you're in the United
  Kingdom, you'll want to visit Sisinghurst, the lifelong passion of
  Vita Sackville-West, and Abbotsford, the obsession of Sir Walter
  Scott. Both are absolutely spectacular, open to the public, and
  worth the off-the-beaten-path side trip.

- **Boston Common:** The Freedom Trail is the central feature of
  the Boston National Historical Park. It includes a self-guided
  tour set up by the National Park Service along nearly three miles
  of the city's labyrinthine streets. It takes visitors through almost
  three centuries of Boston's history from the colonial and revolutionary eras right up to the present, as a red line on the sidewalk

proceeds from site to site. Navigating the warren of streets is never an easy feat—but it is worth the effort. Along the route are several little parks, including the Boston Common. This venerable site is actually America's oldest public park, originally purchased in 1634 by the Puritan settlers as a militia training field and for the feeding of cattle. During the Battle of Bunker Hill the British embarked for Charlestown from the Common. Not only is it a beautiful respite from the bustle of downtown Boston, it is a veritable hive of history.

- **Hartford Colony:** At the turn of the century, Mark Twain called Hartford, Connecticut, home. He once quipped, "Of all the beautiful towns it has been my fortune to see, this is the chief." Most people probably think he was looking out over the wide twists and slow turns of the muddy Mississippi as he wrote his most popular books. In fact, he wrote a good number of them while looking out over the Park River in central Connecticut. The Twain house is a wonderfully colorful brick Victorian mansion built in the midst of a famed artist's colony. It once bristled with creativity. Today, it is a garden of refined New England delights. The place is like a tonic of inspiration—in the same way that a visit to Teddy Roosevelt's Sagamore Hill, Hilaire Belloc's Kings Land, William Faulkner's Rowan Oak, or William Butler Yeats's Thoor Ballylee might be. If you're anywhere near, you'll certainly not want to miss it.

- **Memorial Park:** There are innumerable big city parks that provide citizens with a place for recreation, romance, and refreshment. One of the best is Houston's Memorial Park. Located just adjacent to the sprawling Galleria and Westheimer shopping district and the revitalized Heights neighborhood, it is a cool spate of green in the midst of a hot and humid furor of a city. Magnificent trees, verdant gardens, and wide-open spaces make it a wonderfully civilizing element in the young and restless cityscape.
- **Balboa Park:** There is perhaps no more successful, dynamic, and beautifully planned urban park in all the world than San Diego's Balboa Park. Its rugged terrain, unparalleled zoo, and lush plantings make it a tourist attraction all unto itself. Don't visit Southern California and miss this if there is any way you can help it.

The Herb Garden

An herb garden is a deft combination of the functional and the ornamental. It offers unique variety and color and texture and substance to any environment while simultaneously affording medicinal, culinary, and aromatic benefits as well. For as long as men have made gardens, herbs have been an integral part of them. From vast monastic herbariums and cloisters to little kitchen plots and balcony pots, the cultivation of basil, rosemary, lavender, mint, dill, oregano, cilantro, and a thousand other pungent herbs has been a common occupation delightfully uniting gardeners across every cultural divide.

All my hurts my garden spade can heal.
   RALPH WALDO EMERSON (1803–1882)

Gardening has compensations out of all proportion to its goals. It is creation in the pure sense.
   PHYLLIS MCGINLEY (1905–1978)

To own a bit of ground, to scratch it with a hoe, to plant seeds, and watch the renewal of life—this is the commonest delight of the race, the most satisfactory thing a man can do.
   CHARLES DUDLEY WARNER (1829–1900)

In fine weather the old gentleman is almost constantly in the garden; and when it is too wet to go into it, he will look out of the window at it, by the hour together. He has always something to do there, and you will see him digging, and sweeping, and cutting, and planting, with manifest delight.
   CHARLES DICKENS (1812–1870)

You come to fetch me from my work to-night
When supper's on the table, and we'll see

If I can leave off burying the white
Soft petals fallen from the apple tree.

Soft petals, yes, but not so barren quite,
Mingled with these, smooth bean and wrinkled pea;

And go along with you ere you lose sight
Of what you came for and become like me,

Slave to a springtime passion for the earth.
How Love burns through the Putting in the Seed

On through the watching for that early birth
When, just as the soil tarnishes with weed,

The sturdy seedling with arched body comes
Shouldering its way and shedding the earth crumbs.

ROBERT FROST (1874–1963)

I want death to find me planting my cabbages and herbs.

ᴥ MICHEL DE MONTAIGNE (1533–1592)ᴥ

A good garden may have some weeds—especially if compensated by many herbs.

ᴥ MARK TWAIN (1835–1910) ᴥ

I am convinced that weeds are just herbs we've not found a use for yet.

ᴥ TRISTAN GYLBERD (1954–) ᴥ

A weed is a plant that is not only in the wrong place, but intends to stay, displacing the plant that is in the right place, but is uncertain as to whether it is or it ought.

ᴥ HAROLD GERMAINE (1887–1944) ᴥ

Herbs in my time
Which everyone would praise
Are thrown like weeds
From gardens nowadays.

ᴥ JOHN CLARE (1793–1864) ᴥ

Why is it that the frost hurts not the most unnecessary of weeds, but only the most necessary of herbs?

◦⊦ THOMAS FULLER (1702–1770) ⊦◦

All the pessimism of a Schopenhauer
Is implicit in the garden-lover's creed
That whatever needs attention is an herb
And whatever grows without it is a weed.

◦⊦ MARTHA JOHANNSON (1921–1988) ⊦◦

An herb is a weed you can eat.

◦⊦ BARTELL DESMOND (1899–1968) ⊦◦

Puttering about in my garden, it is the manly herbs, not the effeminate flowers, that afford me the greatest joy. For they radiate energy, fortitude, and vitality. They trojan on through the season. They choke out even the weeds. And they endure well into December. For a gardener, they offer fragrant refreshment and that heady pride that comes with redolent success. I will hereafter, plant only herbs, then.

◦⊦ CHARLES CUPPENHEIMER (1821–1889) ⊦◦

An established herb becomes an heirloom, for in all likelihood it will outlive the gardener who plants it.

◦⊦ ELIZABETH LAWRENCE, C. 1942 ⊦◦

There is no doubt whatsoever that I will be outlived by my garlic, and that long after my own genes have been diluted beyond recognition, my blindweed's genes will be the same genes I left behind in my first, failed herb garden.

SARA STEIN, C. 1988

I used to be ashamed of how much waste there was even in my unpretentious herb garden here. I blamed inexperience, impatience, and extravagance. But now I have come to accept that one must not count the losses, they would be too alarming. One must count only the joys, and feel continually blessed in them. There is no unlucky gardener, for each small success outweighs each defeat in his or her passionate heart.

MARY SARTON, C. 1968

This garden has a soul, I know its moods.

LEIGH HUNT (1784–1859)

There is a calm and certain stay of garden-life.

ROBERT LOUIS STEVENSON (1850–1894)

Gardening, above all crafts, is a matter of faith, grounded however (if on nothing better), on his experience that somehow or other seasons go on in their right course, and bring their right course, and bring their right results.

ᴏᵈ CANON HENRY ELLACOMBE, C. 1897 ᴆ

Herbs don't point a finger. If they live, they don't carry grudges. If they die, unless you've killed an entire species or a rain forest, you feel only momentary guilt, which is quickly replaced by a philosophical, smug feeling: failure is enriching your compost pile.

ᴏᵈ ANN RAVER, C. 1995 ᴆ

One thing that unites all gardeners as they contemplate the compost heap is a belief in reincarnation—at least for plants.

ᴏᵈ GEOFFREY CHARLESWORTH, C. 1988 ᴆ

Artist, creator:
Take thy spade,
It is thy pencil;
Take thy seeds, thy plants,
They are thy colors.

ᴏᵈ WILLIAM MASON (1725–1797) ᴆ

You cannot imagine what a nice walk we had round the orchard. I hear today that an apricot has been detected on one of the trees. But I take it on my own account that the fragrance of the lavender has already begun harkening the advent of spring.

              JANE AUSTEN (1775–1817)

There is nothing very beautiful about the sunflower;
But I am told that it bends toward the sun,
Which is strange and rather appealing.
There is nothing very great about the mustard tree
Yet it is sure that it bears the greatest of all the seeds
And it well describes an eternal kingdom.
How passing strange are such paradoxes
That herbs and plants and seeds should show
The splendor of life and earth and heaven.

              MICAH MCKENTRY (1688–1745)

Hill and Barclay's Hilltop Farm

Visitors were encouraged to touch almost every plant. "Now smell the fragrance," the garden worker would exclaim. It was a heady experience. Butterflies flitted around tiny blossoms and hung on the undersides of leaves. Fat bumblebees flew slowly, lumbering, like military aircraft full of equipment to be delivered. Birds sang from the trees. In the garden beds, rocks cropped up here and there defining spaces, alongside beds marked, "Healing Herbs," "Culinary Herbs," and "Herbs for Potpourri." For the budding herb gardener, Hilltop Herb Farm just outside of Cleveland, Texas, was the best tutorial we could hope for. Perennial herbs like rosemary and mint were present in seemingly infinite varieties. The annuals grew quickly and were pleasingly displayed. An old cart wheel became a divider for a bed, and the pathways meandered along the low hillside, slowing the pace of the student, erudite and novice alike.

That wasn't all, though. After wandering through the garden as a learning experience, visitors could eat in the big garden room. Meals with at least four courses were served, with herbs used in every dish. What could have been a taste cacophony was instead well blended and gentle on the palate. Each course was described, served, and its culinary mysteries revealed as Gwen Hill or Madeline Barclay spoke to the dinner guests. Even the table decorations were herbal.

Finally, one could stroll through the herb shop. Shelves were lined with relishes and preserves, herbal vinegars and oils. An old stove displayed herbal seasoning mixes. Herbal bath products were displayed, and seeds, and books, and gifts. The visitor could spend hours shopping, armed with all the information they had ingested in one short visit.

We visited the Hilltop Herb Farm often when we lived nearby. To get there, you drove north from Houston on a highway, then set off on farm and market roads into the Texas countryside. It was hilly there, and serene. It was hot, humid, and sunny. It was a great place for an herb farm.

Then came the tornado. On May 22, 1987, the sky grew black over the Hilltop Herb Farm. Visitors had begun arriving for dinner even though rain was forecast and their garden tour might be shortened. Any transitional time between seasons in Texas can bring violent weather. May is especially bad. Violent thunderstorms and tornadoes tear around the state as warm, wet air combines with the "northers," or cool fronts, still coming in from the plains north of the state. About one hundred miles from the Gulf of Mexico, Hilltop Herb Farm's turn finally came in a violent attack of weather no one present will ever forget.

It is a miracle that no lives were lost. Visiting even a year afterward, it was obvious that the very ground had been ripped up. The herb beds would never recover. Two of our nation's most learned herb experts would relocate, first far out in the Big Thicket of east Texas, and then to Round Top, in south central Texas, to hang their shingle at a store called "Flavor" where Hill and Barclay reside today.

Round Top is lately known for its antique fairs and is well worth a visit. Anyone visiting should be prepared to continue on to Fredricksburg, to the new location of the Herb Farm just a few blocks from Main Street. The farm is really a cluster of buildings, with shops, a small restaurant, and a day spa. The herb beds are laid out in a large star pattern. Roses intermingle with the lovely herbs, and a windmill stands guard over the whole operation. The Fredricksburg Herb Farm is in the tradition of the old Hilltop Herb Farm, at least from an outsider's viewpoint. They sell seeds, bath and beauty products, and some culinary items. Fredricksburg is well worth a visit not only for the Herb Farm, but also for the fun shopping, unsurpassed German bakeries, and for the Antique Rose Emporium's shop there. But we digress.

We love herbs. We have had various incarnations of herb gardens almost everywhere we've lived, and we've learned all our herb growing lessons the hard way, no matter how much we've read up on things. In fact, rather than learning how to grow things, we seem to learn from the path of learning how not to kill things. Herbs are some of the easiest plants not to kill. They're great for beginners.

But even better, they are the sort of plants that bring unexpected rewards. They're not just hardy survivors, they're fragrant, edible, healthy, medicinal, and often even floral. They're utterly delightful in almost every way imaginable.

There are several categories of herbs. Some fit quite nicely into only one category while some defy precise niches and overlap several. Most have several varieties, which can help when we are trying to locate a particular herb for our climate zone. Some of the categories herbs are typically divided into include:

- **Culinary Herbs:** Basil, oregano, rosemary, thyme, sage, mint, savory, tarragon, sorrel, marjoram, cilantro, lovage, dill, fennel, caraway, and even lavender are popular herbs for the culinary herb garden. These herbs are excellent companion plants for the vegetable garden, discouraging pests and often altering the soil so that the vegetable plant will be healthier and thus resist diseases. For instance, basil is good to plant with tomatoes, dill is good for beans, and rosemary for potatoes. Perhaps the pungency of the companion herbs confuses bugs we don't want in our gardens, or perhaps they taste bad and don't provide a pleasant home for them; whatever the reason, we can tell from personal experience that companion planting works. Herbs such as basil, borage, catnip, hyssop, mints, salvias, oreganos, and thymes attract bees to the garden, which therefore aid in adequate pollination. Since the recent problem with mites in our country's bee population, common honeybees are harder to find than ever. They play a vastly important part in the pollination of our crops, and every gardener should encourage the growth of bee populations by providing host plants and refraining from the use of poisons that might harm them.

- **Medicinal Herbs:** Aloe vera, lavender, echinacea, rosemary, chamomile, catnip, feverfew, lamb's ears, and borage are found among the common medicinal herbs. There are a lot of books out there that relate information about making various tinctures, oils, and poultices with herbs. We don't really mess with that, but we do drink herbal teas when we're under the weather, and use their asceptic properties to stop bleeding and cleanse if we're cut in the garden. More on that later.

- **Herbs for Crafts:** Artemesias, geraniums, lavender, sweet Annie, pennyroyal, salvias, tansy, and yarrow are common herbs used for crafts, most especially wreaths and floral displays. Potpourris are made from lemon balm, lemon verbena, poppies, roses, salvias, tansy, violets, coriander, lavender, mints, and marigolds, among others.

Some gardeners like to plant herbs by theme—such as biblical herb gardens, planted with herbs mentioned in the Bible like dill, horseradish, mustard, rue, mint, and roses. Or perhaps you might prefer to plant your herbs in a Shakespeare garden, with herbs mentioned in the plays of the Bard, such as bay, hyssop, rue, thymes, wormwood, parsley, fennel, and mint.

A good thing to keep in mind when planning an herb garden is the plant's origin. For instance, an herb such as rosemary with Mediterranean origins will desire full sun and low moisture. Plants with spiky or fuzzy leaves will typically fall into this category, like lamb's ears, lavender, and aloe vera.

The ornamental value of herbs ought not be overlooked—an easy trap to fall into since they are so versatile in other ways. But herbs are often very effectively used to set off the color of the flower garden. Silver herbs such as horhound, lamb's ears, sage, rue, "Silver King," "Silver Queen," and "Powys Castle" artemesias are not only lovely used in the flower garden to calm the effect of bright color, but are spectacular in the white garden or used with blue, such as Victoria Blue Salvia or baptisia, and interplanted with roses. A lovely fern-leafed fennel plant is a wonderful underplanting for rosebushes, as is yarrow or dill.

The design of herb beds is typically different from that of flower or vegetable gardens. Herbs are sometimes simply interplanted among flowers and vegetables, as in our own gardens, or they are planted in well-designed, usually small, beds that show them off as specimens. Here the fuzzy lines between flowers and herbs, and herbs and weeds, are usually evident. Herbs may be planted in knot gardens, emphasizing the green, yellow, and silver foliage of the plants—the peculiar contribution of the Celts to the gardening legacy of the Western world. In these gardens, the plants are laid out in geometric designs, but require frequent trimming to be especially effective. Germander, artemesias, boxwood, and santolina are commonly found in the knot garden.

If you live in the city, perhaps even in an apartment, herb gardening is still a possibility for you. When we were in graduate school, we squeezed our family into innumerable tiny rental spaces and ticky-tacky apartment complexes. But we were never without our herbs and flowers. Indeed, we can hardly imagine life without them. And we're convinced that once you get started, you will feel the same way.

A Practicum on Herbals

An herbal is any use of herbs, or mixtures of herbs for human purposes—not just in medicines, but in foods and in aromatics as well. Here are some of our favorite herbal recipes:

- We always make iced tea with mint. We live in the South, so we have firm opinions on how tea should be made. First, while water is boiling, we pour almost a cupful of sugar into a pitcher. We slice up about half a lemon and put it in with the sugar. We cut some mint and rinse it well, then smash it into the sugar. When the water has come to a boil, we pour it into the pitcher and use three family-sized Luzianne tea bags for our half gallon of tea. There usually isn't much left, but if there is, we take out the mint if the tea will sit overnight. It's good.

- We also like basil. If we're good and harvest all our basil before the first frost in October, we make plenty of pesto, and freeze it in small batches. Here's the recipe we use:

2 cloves garlic, peeled	¾ c freshly grated Parmesan cheese
½ t salt	¼ c freshly grated Romano cheese
2 c tightly packed basil leaves	5 T butter, softened
5 T roasted pine nuts	
½ c olive oil	

  We wash, rinse, and dry the basil. Then we roast the pine nuts in the oven for a little while, just till lightly browned. Or, this can be done in a cast-iron skillet. Then into the blender go the garlic, salt, basil, nuts, and olive oil. Purée. Next, add the cheeses and butter, pulsing briefly. Add hot water if the pesto is too thick. Serve on the side. Just a little is a fine accompaniment to pasta.

- For variety, we like to make cilantro pesto, substituting cilantro for the basil and pecans for the pine nuts. We have also made a mint pesto as an accompaniment to lamb. Think of strong-flavored herbs and garlic with a pinch of salt, nuts, cheese, and oil, and you will come up with some great pestos that fit well with your favorite dishes.

- Another very simple flavoring is lavender sugar. When laboriously harvesting lavender flowers from your lavender plants, set aside some of the stems to use for lavender sugar and for herbes de provence. Both seasoning mixtures are quite unique, and it is great to have them available in your kitchen. Simply rinse the lavender stems lightly and strip the flowers into a bowl. Lavender is very pungent, so sparingly add around 4 to 5 tablespoons of the flowers to a quart of sugar. I like to use a quart jar. Shake it well, and take the lid off for a few minutes daily and give it a shake so that the moisture can escape. This sugar is wonderful in cheesecake or shortbread.

- When cooking with fresh herbs, it is important to remember that fresh herbs are not as pungent as dried, so you must use them in larger amounts when fresh. When adding to a soup or stew, add dried herbs during cooking, and fresh herbs near the last. Fresh herb leaves are always a welcome addition to salads, stews, soups, and vegetables. Fresh dill in potato salad is great, as well as on fish.

- We like to make herbal vinegars, too. They're so simple to make, and they provide flavored vinegars for cooking and for making vinaigrettes all year long. Simply wash one or a variety of companionable herbs and let them air dry. Place them into the bottom of a fruit jar while heating vinegar on the stove. Do not bring the vinegar to a boil. Pour the warmed vinegar over the herbs, and strain in two or three weeks' time. Our favorites include tarragon vinegar made with apple cider vinegar; thyme, oregano, and rosemary vinegar made with red wine vinegar; and raspberry vinegar made by soaking fresh raspberries in white vinegar for a few days, then straining. Raspberry vinegar isn't herbal, but it's sure good. We also use herbal vinegars in cooking. If we caramelize onions, for instance, we always pour in a splash of balsamic or herb-flavored vinegar along with a couple of teaspoons of sugar. Herbal vinegars are good splashed in tiny doses on beef while it's cooking, and in vegetable dishes. We always use tarragon vinegar in deviled eggs and potato salad. Try your own concoctions! Read the ingredients on the bottles of herbal vinegars at your local supermarket, and grow and make your own creations from your herb garden.

The Cottage Garden

The cottage garden is a distinctively English art form. Often cramped into tiny spaces and tucked under the eaves of city houses or walkups, cottage gardens nevertheless are marvelously expressive and expansive. They are generally relaxed, natural, and more than a little muddled. There are no master plans, really. Neither are there rhymes or reasons. But they all seem to work quite nicely together anyway. Their wholes are always more than the sums of their parts. They convey a sense that they belong, that they are indigenous parts of their environment. They are comfortable. They are accessible. They are like . . . well, they are rather like the homes they so graciously complement—there is just something immediately recognizable, personal, and inviting about them.

To prevent undue disappointment, those who wish for beautiful flower borders and whose enthusiasm is greater than their knowledge, should be reminded that if a border is to be planted for pictorial effect, it is impossible to maintain that effect and to have the space well filled for any period longer than three months. . . . It should also be borne in mind that a good hardy flower border cannot be made all at once.

◀ GERTRUDE JEKYLL (1843–1932) ▶

Every experienced Christian gardener knows that there is a spiritual spring which comes just as surely as nature's spring. The Lenten spring is God's invitation to prayer, fasting, and penance. Like the deep-rooted thistle weed, some of our worst habits withstand all but the most persistent, persevering, and strenuous exercise. A quick pull on the root, however, will not do the trick, nor will an aggressive chop of the hoe. Patience is needed, and the humble willingness to drop down on one's knees and work carefully with the hand fork and trowel. The Christian gardener patiently picks sin from the soul's soil and cultivates it with care and attention to the tender new growth of faith. The Christian gardener also respects the fact that God appoints each soul to be "the sort of garden it is to be." "Your job," Underhill admonishes, "is strictly confined to making [your soul] as good as it can be of its sort." Some of us will be contemplative in the manner of a rose garden, and others are more earthy and restless, like a potato patch.

❧ VIGEN GUROIAN, C. 1999 ❧

Now hath flora rob'd her bowers
To befriend this place with flowers;
Strowe about, strowe about
The sky rayn'd never kindlier showers.

           ⊰ THOMAS CAMPION (1567–1620) ⊱

There is nothing in the world more peaceful than the dappling of
light through the leaves of my cottage garden's apple tree with an
early moon.

           ⊰ ALICE MEYNELL (1847–1922) ⊱

Under the window, on a dusty ledge,
He peers among the spider webs for seed.
He wonders, groping, if the spiders spun
Beneath that window after all. Perhaps
His eyes are spiders, and new veils are dropped
Each winter and summer morning in the brain.
He sees but silken-dimly, though the ends
Of his white fingers feel more things than are:
More delicate webs, and sundry bags of seed.
That flicker at the window is a wren.
She taps the pane with a neat tail, and scolds.
He knows her there, and hears her—far away,
As if an insect sang in a tree. Whereat
The shelf he fumbles on is distant, too,
And his bent arm is longer than an arm.
Something between his fingers brings him back:
An envelope that rustles, and he reads:
"The coreopsis." He does not delay.
Down from the rafter where they always hang
He shoulders rake and hoe, and shuffles out.

The sun is warm and thick upon the path,
But he goes lightly, under a broad straw
None knows the age of. They are watching him
From upper windows as his slippered feet
Avoid the aster and nasturtium beds
Where he is not to meddle. His preserve
Is further, and no stranger touches it.
Yesterday he was planting larkspur there.
He works the ground, he hoes the larkspur out,
Pressing the coreopsis gently in.
With an old hose he plays a quivering stream,
Then shuffles back with the tools and goes to supper.

Over his bowl of milk, wherein he breaks
Five brittle crackers, drifts the question, "Uncle,
What have you planted for the summer coming?"
"Why—hollyhocks," he murmurs, and they smile.

ܘ MARK VAN DOREN (1894–1972) ܘ

I count my blessings with the flowers, never with the leaves that fall.

❧ LADY BIRD JOHNSON (1912–) ☙

In front of the house the long borders have been stocked with lark-
spurs, annual and perennial, columbines, giant poppies, pinks,
Madonna lilies, wall flowers, hollyhocks, perennial phloxes, peonies,
lavender, starworts, cornflowers, Lychnis chalcedonica, and bulbs
packed in wherever bulbs could go. These are the borders that were
so hardly used by the other gardener.

❧ ELIZABETH VON ARNIM, C. 1955 ☙

On the warm, moon-clear May nights we like to sit out in the Quiet
Garden. I call it a Quiet Garden, because it is filled with quiet old-
fashioned flowers and herbs—a place to be tranquil in. In one corner, the old crooked apple tree is drifted with the white miracle of
apple blossoms. The low white picket fence which encloses the small
flagged area is half hidden by the young green of the rambler roses.
The herbs are up; the lavender came through the bitter winter
safely.

❧ GLADYS TABER, C. 1967 ☙

I think I may be a better person for having given serious time and thought and effort to gardening. I am proud of having learned to work with nature to encourage beauty in my backyard. The hours I have spent cultivating the soil, weeding and planting, and just looking at what has come to be have given me boundless pleasure. I no longer say, as I once did, "I have to work in the garden today." I say, with deep contentment, "I'm gardening today." I have truly reaped the bounty of the garden.

꙰ MARTHA STEWART, C. 1998 ꙰

Would you not consider a person foolish and absurd, who should extravagantly love and prize a drop of stagnant water, and yet view the ocean with indifference or disgust? Or who should constantly grovel in the dust to admire a shining grain of sand, yet neglect to admire the sun which caused it to shine? Of what folly and absurdity then are we guilty, when we love the imperfectly amiable qualities of our fellow worms, or admire the sublimity and beauty of the works of nature, and yet exercise no love to him to whom they are indebted for all; him whose glory gilds the heavens, and from whom angels derive every thing that can excite admiration or love.

꙰ EDWARD PAYSON, C. 1830 ꙰

How magnificent it sounds! That is the fun of writing of one's cottage garden: a steep bank can be a cliff, a puddle a pool, a pool a lake, bog and moraine sound as though a guide were needed to find your way across them, and yet may be covered by a sheet of the Times. My dolomites lie within the compass of my outstretched arms.

᥍ EDWARD AUGUSTUS BOWLES (1865–1954) ᥈

He leaped a fence and saw that all nature was a garden.

᥍ HORACE WALPOLE (1717–1797) ᥈

What wondrous life is this I lead!
Ripe apples drop about my head;
The luscious clusters of the vine
Upon my mouth do crush their wine;
The nectarine and curious peach
Into my hands themselves do reach;
Stumbling on melons, as I pass,
Ensnared with flowers, I fall on grass.
Meanwhile the mind, from pleasure less,
Withdraws in happiness:
The mind, that ocean, where each kind
Does straight its own resemblance find;
Yet it creates, transcending these,
Far other worlds, and other seas,
Annihilating all that's made
To a green thought in a green shade.

ANDREW MARVELL (1621–1678)

Inspiration is the bottom line. Without it the first move could not be made. We need to be led on bit by bit, by visits to gardens private and public, by garden tours, by immersing ourselves in illustrated garden books and catalogues. We see, absorb, winnow, and sift, and finally our imaginations take wing and out of all this come our gardening plans.

ᴏⱠ Emily Whaley, c. 1997 Ɑᴏ

POTTER'S MONK CONISTON ESTATE

The view is framed through the arbor arching over the garden gate. The pathway is curved, and the vegetation cultivated, yet somewhat left to its own sense of direction. Such is the typical illustration of a cottage garden in Beatrix Potter's (1866–1943) works. We view from inside the gate, from a low, natural perspective. While Potter's larger body of work ranged from lovely landscapes to her carefully executed drawings of fungi for scientific studies, the public remains most familiar with her lovely illustrations of things most familiar.

Tommy Tittlemouse munches on grains of wheat in Potter's 1905 *Book of Rhymes.* His nest forms the background of the illustration, and grass blades interspersed with tiny flowers form the foreground. Toadstools become chairs for outdoor picnics. Kittens walk along paths toward stone cottages past roses, salvias, and carnations in *The Tale of Tom Kitten.* Foxgloves, hollyhocks, and pansies hold the kittens' attention. Potter masterfully used the familiar cottage garden as the backdrop for her masterful children's tales. In such familiar settings, who could say that ducks weren't conversing with foxes, or kittens with mice, or rabbits with piglets? When drawn in such familiar surroundings, anything can seem possible, especially when we want it to be. As any science fiction writer with outlandish tales to tell knows well, the more familiar the setting, the more believable the story. If pigs use walking sticks and wear bow ties and waistcoats, they do seem rather more inclined to converse in cultured syllables, although they still exhibit piggish desires.

If Mrs. Tittlemouse was to be believable, she should therefore sleep in a little box bed, as did cottage-dwellers in the Lake District where Potter visited whenever possible and made her home in her later years. Potter's characters should water their flowers and tend their gardens, always wear aprons in the kitchen, and scrub their faces if their intended audience was to be wooed into the realm of the plausible.

Although better examples of quintessential cottage gardens might be found elsewhere, it is this use of the cottage garden as setting that appeals to us. For in reality, that is what makes it so attractive to us. After all, is it much more of a stretch to attempt to replicate an English cottage garden in August in Tennessee than it is to animate that garden with the personalities in Potter's books? The cottage garden is, to our way of thinking, more of a setting than an exact science.

The same point can be made by observing the living room in anyone's home. Now, let's not quibble about whether it is a sitting room, a den, a family room, or a screened porch. Find the room where we go to read, spend time with our guests, and relax, and observe its characteristics. What are the primary characteristics of the room? Is it the television, with seating arranged around this altar? Is the area set up for comfortable conversation, or game-playing, or reading? Or is the room slightly uncomfortable, but extremely impressive in value and size of furnishings? Is there a fireplace? Are there paintings? If so, is there a theme in them? What books inhabit the shelves? Are they only for display, or mostly reference works for educational pursuits, or do we find mysteries, biographies, and "how to" books?

Answering these questions tells us a lot about the house's inhabitants. Is the desire to impress visitors, or to make guests comfortable? Is one drawn into the room to curl up for conversation, or impressed with the discreet assemblage of fine things? Can both fineness and comfort coexist? If so, how?

In this way, we can see that the cottage garden personifies the comfortable, somewhat laissez-faire, naturalistic leanings of its owners just as the cookie-cutter plantings left by suburban contractors personify the owner who simply wants to fit in. Do most people even put this much thought into their gardens? Probably not. Our point, exactly.

What distinguishes a cottage garden from "three flowerbeds, boxwood underplanting, and a lovely rosebush"? According to Gabrielle van Zuylen's *The Garden, Visions of Paradise*, cottage gardens can be defined as "the simple, unpretentious gardens of small homes in rural England, their seemingly casual plantings, often with old-fashioned flowers, greenery, vegetables and trees. . . ."

Cottage gardens should be enclosed for best effect. Whether the enclosure be natural, such as hedges, wooden pickets or fieldstone, or man-made, like forged-iron fencing, it both sets off and contains the riotous plantings one finds inside. In Potter's stories, traveling outside the immediate garden to the cottage or dwelling place of the characters represents possible danger, or wilderness. It is the habitation of foxes, of wolves, of the unknown. This is not at all to imply that Potter confined her settings to cottage gardens; it is to say that when she employed their use as setting, they represented home, comfort, and safety. This is what they still convey.

Beatrix Potter was the only daughter born to Rupert and Helen Potter, a middle-class couple in Kensington. Her family was comfortable enough to employ servants, and as was typical in Victorian England, Beatrix was left to her nursery maid's charge. Her only sibling, Bertram, was born six years later. Beatrix and Bertram lived secluded lives, even for their time and class. Happily for the two children, the family routinely escaped from the city to the Scottish highlands, and later the northern Lake District in England for the summer. Both children came to love the wildlife, flora, and fauna in the countryside. As her parents discouraged the formation of close friendships for both children, they found themselves with more time than most children for individual pursuits, such as drawing and writing. When Bertram went off to boarding school, Beatrix stayed behind for tutoring from her governess. By the time she was a teenager, painting for Beatrix had become a passion.

The Potter family continued to spend holidays in rented homes in the countryside. It was on one of these trips to Scotland, write biographers Judy Taylor, Irene Whalley, Anne Stevenson Hobbs, and Elizabeth M. Battrick, "that Beatrix wrote the letter to five-year-old Noel Moore that was to become one of the most famous letters ever written. It began, 'My dear Noel, I don't know what to write to you, so I shall tell you a story about four little rabbits whose names were Flopsy, Mopsy, Cottontail and Peter.'"

Potter took art lessons and, increasingly, her adroitness in depictions of nature was recognized, if not rewarded by recognition. In fact, according to her biographers, a carefully prepared paper, "On the Germination of the Spores of Agaricineae" was "presented to the Linnean Society of London, not by Beatrix, as ladies were not allowed to attend the Society's meetings, but by the very man at Kew who had earlier been so dismissive of her claims."

Beatrix's family friend Hardwicke Rawnsley urged her to publish her spectacularly illustrated children's stories so enjoyed by the Moore family. After Beatrix self-published *The Tale of Peter Rabbit*, the book was picked up in 1902 by the Norman Warne publishing company and became literally an instant success. *The Tale of Squirrel Nutkin* and *The Tailor of Gloucester* followed on its heels by Christmas of 1903.

Beatrix and Bertram's personal lives continued to be somewhat lonely. Discouraged from matrimony, Beatrix nevertheless determined to marry her publisher, Norman Warne. But before she had the chance, he died of pernicious anemia. She was left with the shock of the sudden death of a loved one as well as the prospect of a lifetime of care for her aging parents. Bertram secretly married. Seven years later, Bertram revealed his own secret marriage to his parents, so when Beatrix fell in love with William Heelis in 1913, she too was allowed to marry.

Along with World War I came the news that Harold Warne's forgeries had nearly ruined the Warne publishing company. Potter was never paid all the thousands of pounds in royalties due her. She stuck with the company, publishing more and more books to help them regain solvency and thus begin to repay her lost earnings. During this time, she and her husband settled in the Lake District. He commuted from Hawkshead for a time while Beatrix, now her mother's sole caretaker, built up their farms and livestock pursuits. Her mother lived near them and died of old age in 1932.

By this time Beatrix Potter's books were published by an American publisher in Philadelphia, David McKay, as well as by Frederick Warne in England. She was finally able to use her considerable income to accomplish her own dreams; she purchased more land in the Lake District and carefully managed it, working all the while with the National Trust to preserve the Monk Coniston Estate for transfer to them upon her death.

Beatrix Potter Heelis and her husband never had children, but she cared for and entertained both her husband's relations and her own, pursued the breeding of Herdwick sheep for showing (she became president of the Herdwick Sheepbreeder's Association), and contributed to the welfare of her local community by setting up local health-care centers. In later life, she published fewer and fewer books, instead pursuing her beloved occupation of farming and livestock management. She died before the end of World War II, in December of 1943, her husband at her side.

Although Beatrix Potter Heelis was a large landholder and certainly not a cottager, her lifetime appreciation of the cottage and all it represented became a mission in her later years. She purchased land and cottages in the Lake District whenever possible, solely for the purpose of preservation of a way of life and the land. Her depictions of the cottage garden in her published children's works are still some of the best representations of the style in both Victorian and Edwardian England. Those of us who emulate this style of garden can still learn much from Beatrix Potter Heelis.

A Practicum on Seed-Saving

We love to spend January leafing through seed catalogs. They begin to arrive at our house in early January, build up a good head of steam during the spring, and begin to slack off in the summertime.

When the leaves are falling in the autumn, a few gardening catalogs drift down to us as well, full mostly of flower arrangements and garden-related stuff we might want to purchase for Christmas gifts, or things that didn't sell during the growing season and are on sale.

Around planting time wherever you live, area feed stores, discount stores, garden shops, nurseries, and gift shops stock seeds. If we have purchased our seeds by mail, we can't look at these displays. If we do, we'll break down and buy new varieties. This blows our seed-buying budget, but we do always seem to find a few things we really need but forgot to order ahead. The feed stores are especially good places to hunt down varieties of vegetables that grow well in your area. They may not be old-fashioned varieties, but they will grow in the local soil, within the confines of the local weather, and are available for local farmers and home gardeners alike.

There's another way to procure seeds, though. You can save your own. When your own flowers are finished blooming, they will have heads full of seeds that you can harvest to plant. We always leave a few for the birds, especially of purple coneflower, rudbeckia, and always sunflowers, but it is worth letting your own seeds dry a little on the stalk, then save them for next year. There are some real advantages to harvesting your own seeds. First, you know they grow well in your own climate. If a plant has performed very poorly or has been eaten up by insects or looks sickly, you don't pick seeds from it. Go only to healthy, good producers. Find the best specimens from within your own garden, and take seeds from these flowers. Second, these seeds are free. The cheapest seeds you can find are about a dollar per bag, and you can have these for nothing. Third, you know the exact color and growth pattern of the flowers these seeds will produce. But be careful! If these plants are some sort of hybrid, they will not reproduce in kind. The seeds you harvest from them will revert back to a parent plant. You must know your own plants before you know whether to harvest the seeds or not. On the other hand, if you're not sure, it doesn't cost you anything to experiment with it and see what comes up from them next year.

Now, you don't have to pick seeds from perennials unless you want to plant some in another place in your garden or share them with a friend. Perennials will come back by themselves. If you plant annuals, or biennials, however, you may want to be sure to harvest some seeds so you don't have to purchase them at all next planting season.

When you harvest the seeds, lay them out on a paper towel for a couple of days to let them dry out well. Some people then place them in a Mason jar, some place them in resealable baggies, and Martha Stewart probably has some gloriously beautiful seed-saver kits that come with little paper bags you can label yourself, for only a small charge. If you're the Martha type, you could go to a stationery store and purchase tiny envelopes, label them, line them up alphabetically, and store them in a vintage tin with a special label,

"Seeds, Summer 2001." Our method is to put them in resealable baggies. We do label the bags with the following information: plant name, color if necessary, season, and year. If we want to be organized, we toss them into a shoebox in the freezer.

Plantsmen differ about whether or not seeds must be frozen in storage. Obviously, before freezing methods were invented, seeds were stored and used for the next year's harvest. The important thing is that they not be subjected to extremely high temperatures or to humidity, because germination could begin before you plant them. So, although freezing isn't mandatory, seeds will last for years this way, and you will probably have a better germination ratio than if they are stored at room temperature.

Last year we were on the "garden economy plan," along with a gardening friend. We didn't allow ourselves to buy many seeds at all, but instead shared the old seeds we had stored in our freezers and had put carefully away in the back of a drawer until some growing season now long past. We had a great germination rate from the seeds stored in the freezer, even those that had been in there for years. Seeds stored at room temperature for more than a couple of years also germinated fairly well. Seeds stored in a potting shed or in a garage did not germinate well. They had been exposed to very high temperatures here during our southern summers. Hollyhock and cosmos seed harvested by a gardener friend and stored at room temperature for a year in her kitchen germinated beautifully as well.

It was fun to use up the leftover seeds from half-used bags and to share seeds and plants between friends. We also attended local garden club sales for perennials and herbs and bought some healthy, unusual specimens at great prices, but had to deal with large crowds. On the other hand, crowds at garden club sales aren't exactly comparable to crowds at the football stadium or at a sale at the mall. The garden club crowd conversation goes something like this:

"Oops, sorry."

"Oh, me too. Ooh, what do you have there?"

"*Umph!* This is some sort of really cool black aster that's supposed to have lovely dark foliage all summer, then tiny pinky-white flowers in the early fall."

"Really! Uh—sorry, was that your foot? Here, let me hold that while you pick that up. So where did you get that aster?"

"Over there, in the corner where those anemones were that everyone wanted."

"Oh, thanks. Have fun!"

These local garden club crowds are really tough. On the other hand, we were fortunate enough to attend the Chelsea Garden Show in London one year. It was the absolute fulfillment of a dream. The flowers were exquisite, the plants both rare and beautiful, and the garden vignettes fabulous. The crowd, however, was different.

"Oops, sorry."

"Sorry."

"My, this is beautiful, isn't it?"

Blank stare.

"Quite a crowd, huh?"

Blank stare, with obvious thought process: *American. Chatty. Ignore her and maybe she'll get the message.*

I suppose I got the message, but it certainly wasn't as much fun without sharing.

The Flower Garden

When most folks think of gardening, they think of flowers. And well they should. Flowers are bright, colorful, beautiful, stunningly varied, fragrant, and immensely gratifying. A springtime spray of reds, violets, yellows, blues, pinks, whites, and every hue in between invigorates the heart and inspires the hands of the gardener like nothing else in this world. How much art, music, literature, philosophy, architecture, and theology has been inspired by flowers? It would be impossible to tell, but the fact that beauty and flowers, love and flowers, kindness and flowers, consolation and flowers, faith and flowers, and victory and flowers are all inextricably linked says something about the universal appeal of flowers.

Flowers have a mysterious and subtle influence upon the feelings, not unlike some strains of music. They relax the tenseness of the mind. They dissolve its rigor.

ৰ‌ HENRY WARD BEECHER (1813–1877) ‌৹

There is more beauty in a single flower than could adorn all the greatest cathedrals in the world.

ৰ‌ JOHN RUSKIN (1819–1900) ‌৹

Flower in the crannied wall
I pluck you out of the crannies
I hold you here, root and all, in my hand
Little flower—but if I could understand
What you are, root and all, and all in all
I should know what God and man is.

ৰ‌ ALFRED, LORD TENNYSON (1809–1892) ‌৹

There was never mystery
But 'tis figured in the flowers;
Was never secret history
But birds tell it in the bowers.

ৰ‌ RALPH WALDO EMERSON (1803–1882) ‌৹

We live among marvels: each flower a masterpiece of subtle beauty, form, and scent.

ⲟᵻ MARION GARRETTY (1917–1996) ᵻⲟ

The Amen! of nature is always a flower.

ⲟᵻ OLIVER WENDELL HOLMES (1809–1894) ᵻⲟ

It would be idle to deny that those gardens contained flarze in full measure. They were bright with Achillea, Bignonia Radicans, Campanula, Digitalis, Euphorbia, Funkia, Gypsophilia, Helianthus, Iris, Liatris, Monarda, Phlox Drummindii, Salvia, Thalictrum, Vinca, and Yucca. But the devil of it was that Angus McAlister, the gardener, would have had a fit if they were picked.

ⲟᵻ P. G. WODEHOUSE (1881–1975) ᵻⲟ

Go, lovely rose,
Tell her that wastes her time and me,
That now she knows,
When I resemble her to thee,
How sweet and fair she seems to be.

            ENMUND WALLER (1606–1687)

Flowers are the sweetest things God ever made and forgot to put a soul into.

            HENRY WARD BEECHER (1813–1887)

There is no such thing as an ordinary flower.

            CHARLOTTE GRAY (1928–)

The rose is a rose,
And always was a rose
But the theory goes
That the apple's a rose
And the pear is, and so's
The plum, I suppose.
The dear only knows
What will next prove a rose.
You, of course, are a rose:
But were always a rose.

ROBERT FROST (1874–1963)

We cannot fathom the mystery of a single flower, nor is it intended that we should; but that the pursuit of science should constantly be betrayed by the love of beauty, and accuracy of knowledge by the tenderness of emotion.

JOHN RUSKIN (1819–1900)

'Tis the last rose of summer
Left blooming alone;
All her lovely companions
Are faded and gone;
No flower of her kindred,
No rosebud is nigh,
To reflect back her blushes,
To give sigh for sigh.

I'll not leave thee, thou lone one!
To pine on the stem;
Since the lovely are sleeping,
Go, sleep thou with them.
Thus kindly I scatter
Thy leaves o'er the bed,
Where thy mates of the garden
Lie scentless and dead.

So soon may I follow,
When friendships decay,
And from Love's shining circle
The gems drop away.
When true hearts lie withered
And fond ones are flown,
Oh! Who would inhabit
This bleak world alone?
           ❧ THOMAS MOORE (1779–1852) ❧

In eastern lands they talk in flowers and tell in a garland their loves
and cares.
           ❧ JAMES GATES PERCIVAL (1795–1856) ❧

A rosebud by my early walk,
Adown a corn-enclosed bawk,
Saw gently bent its thorny stalk,
All on a dewy morning.
Ere twice the shades o' dawn stir glory,
In a' its crimson glory spread,
And drooping rich the dewy head,
It scents the early morning.

Within the bush, her covert nest,
A little linnet fondly prest;
The dew sat chilly on her breast
Sae early in the morning.
She soon shall see her tender brood,
The pride, the pleasure o' the wood,
Amang the fresh green leaves bedewed,
Awake the early morning.

So thou, dear bird, young Jeany fair!
On trembling string, or vocal air,
Shall sweetly pay the tender care
That tends thy early morning.
So thou, sweet rosebud, young and gay,
Shalt beauteous blaze upon the day,
And bless the parent's evening ray
That watched thy early morning.

ROBERT BURNS (1759–1796)

A flower unplucked is but left to the falling, and nothing is gained by not gathering roses.

ROBERT FROST (1874–1963)

Won't you come into my garden? I want my roses to see you.
⟨ RICHARD SHERIDEN (1751–1816) ⟩

A morning glory at my window satisfies me more than the meta-
physics of books.
⟨ WALT WHITMAN (1819–1892) ⟩

I have a garden of my own
But so with roses overgrown,
And lilies, that you would it guess
To be a little wilderness.
⟨ ANDREW MARVELL (1621–1678) ⟩

If there were commandments associated with organic gardening, the first and greatest of these would be "Honor thy soil!" Care of the roses themselves must take second place to care of the soil in which they grow if you want a healthy garden. Most of us are not gifted with perfect garden soil, which would be equal parts sand, topsoil, and organic material. But good soil is, literally, the basis of all good gardening and an absolute requirement for good organic gardening. You can scrounge your plants, scavenge your building materials, even forget to fertilize now and then, but the one part of gardening to which everyone should sincerely pay attention is in the development and maintenance of the soil.

ᴏᖨ LIZ DRUITT, C. 1982 ᖨᴏ

Who loves a garden
Still his Eden keeps,
Perennial pleasures plants,
And wholesome harvest reaps.

ᴏᖨ BRONSON ALCOTT (1799–1888) ᖨᴏ

CHURCHILL'S CHARTWELL

Flappers danced wildly, and money was easy to be had. Their skirts shortened, they smoked and used slang calculated to shock. The Great War was over, and right had won out. Sleek automobiles flew past cartloads of hay in the countryside. Veterans, gasping for breath since deadly fog over foreign trenches had poisoned the rest of their lives, bided time outside village shops.

Clementine planted roses in a walled garden.

Those who had leadership roles during wartime craved the opposite of mad 1920s society. The louder and brighter it got, the less enchanting the gilt to those who wrote the letters: "Dear Mr. and Mrs. Smythe: It is with deep regret that I write this letter to confirm the death of your dear son Arthur. As you know, he fell in Flanders, but I wanted to write to you and tell you of his bravery, especially in the days leading up to his death. His fellow soldiers were fond of him, and asked me to write you with these recollections. . . ."

Winston wrote many of those letters. He also wrote policy-making letters and took unpopular stands, lost Parliament seats and regained them. He smoked, drank, hardly slept, and played "Gorilla" with his children. He built them a tree house, and his smallest daughter, Mary, a little play cottage of her own near the garden, called the "Marycot."

Like Ulysses, the Churchills had seen all the wonders of the world. They traveled extensively throughout North America, Europe, Africa, the Middle East, and Central and South America. They enjoyed their stays amid the hustle and bustle of the world's greatest cities. And they relished their opportunities to tramp about in the world's most untamed wildernesses. But their lifelong conviction was that for all the majesty, splendor, and mystery of those distant realms, there was no place like home.

They made their home in the Kent countryside south of London a haven of rest from the hurly-burly of public life. They both found solace there. The demands of leadership necessitated a place they could call home, a place where they could rest, a place where they could recuperate from the constant wrangling of politics.

It was there that the Churchills employed secretaries, butlers, gardeners, a chauffeur, maids, and cooks. They entertained often. Through the years the house served as a mecca for the distinguished men of the age. It was the meeting place for all those whose ideas, actions, and intentions animated the time with optimism and confidence. Scientists, naturalists, thinkers, writers, artists, statesmen, reformers, and businessmen gathered there to imbibe of the atmosphere and to sit in the proximity of their greatest champion and mentor.

When duty called them away, they always longed to return. And when they did return, they returned with all their hearts.

After the Second World War, Winston's talents were unappreciated. The country was ready for a change, and he was unceremoniously not reelected after the war. He poured his frustration, his sorrow, his energy, and all his pent-up longings for home into Chartwell, which remained faithful. He helped build rockeries and waterfalls and little ponds stuffed with fat goldfish. He oversaw building and remodeling projects, and built walls. Brick by brick he built, slathering mortar carefully, chomping on a cigar, enlisting the help of a child or a visitor to hand him the next brick to be placed carefully, thoughtfully, until a row was completed, perfectly aligned.

And Clementine gardened. Her rose garden had walls all around it and she planted the four squares with tea roses. Along the beds inside the walls, she planted pastel-colored flowers, including penstemons and catmint. Her cousin Venetia Montagu advised her on the garden's design, knowing Clemmie's tastes were simple, her method quiet, her taste impeccable. The scent of the tea roses filled her house when they were in bloom; she always had fresh flowers in the house.

For their golden anniversary, the Churchills received from their children the "Golden Rose Walk," a lovely single pathway with an elliptical center with sundial. The rose walk was hedged in yew, with gold and yellow roses of all kinds between the pathway and the hedge. It says a lot about the Churchills that a rose walk is the greatest gift their own children could think of for these parents who modeled courage, fortitude, and faith during the most trying times in modern British and world history.

We actually avoided growing roses for a number of years, because we were a little afraid of their reputation. Aside from the lovely rosebush from our tenth wedding anniversary we had to leave behind when we moved, we shied away from the attempt. Part of the reason, too, was that we are organic gardeners, and in the South the general assumption is that you must water and spray, spray and water, and then water and spray a little to have beautiful roses. We sighed when we visited the rose gardens at Chartwell and other lovely gardens. We were uninformed. We had dozens of other kinds of flowers. But no roses.

Now we know better. And roses have become a major focus of our gardens.

Rose growers generally fall into two camps: organic and organic-is-stupid. Imagine our surprise when we found that not only are there roses that grow best in southern climates, there are even those that resist disease enough to get by without spraying. Now, let's be clear from the beginning: that rosarian's backyard in the town garden show with the saucer-sized buds of every color all in continuous bloom with not a black spot on a leaf to be found, that guy's in the organic-is-stupid camp—and it makes me mad just to talk about it. His roses will take your breath away. Unfortunately, they will also take the breath from a few other creatures that are part of the balance of nature. But his roses as a whole can be showstoppers.

Now, own-root, non-hybrid roses that are carefully chosen for your own climate zone can be spectacular as well. If they are planted in good soil with compost and watered well, like any plant grown in an organic garden system, you just won't have many problems with insects or disease. The truth of the matter is, a healthy plant can resist a little chewing on and a little black spot, just as a healthy person won't catch every virus that comes around, while someone with a suppressed immune system will have frequent bouts with disease. This person must rely on antibiotics and other miracles of modern medicine that we are glad to have around. However, just as an over-reliance on antibiotics is producing frighteningly strong bacterium, an over-reliance on poisons in the garden will encourage weaker and weaker plant life.

We have roses from our own local nursery, and we have them from mail-order nurseries, and all of them seem to do well as long as we water them well and they have great soil. Roses have a reputation for being extremely picky. They like plenty of nutrition, which for them means fertilizer. These are some things that should help ensure rose-growing success at your house:

- Plant roses in late fall or early spring. Your own climate will guide you in the depth of the hole and how far up you bring the soil around your rose. Basically, dig the hole deep enough for the roots to have a little wiggle room at the bottom and the soil to come up around the crown of the plant (that knobby thing at the top of the roots). In spring, pull the soil away from the crown. Put some bone meal and compost or the fertilizer of your choice in the soil as you refill the hole. Now water it and look for growth.

- Water your roses often. You could give them a gallon of water each day, and they would love you for it. We can get by with once every two to three days in the summer and less in cooler weather. We don't water at all in the winter.

- In early spring, prune back about one-third of climbing roses so that every three years you have completely new canes. Otherwise, prune off dead or diseased portions of the bush. Don't over-prune. You might keep it pruned during the summer, but not after late summer.

- Something that encourages a lot of blooming is to pull branches of climbers laterally and tie them down, as along a fence or on an arbor. Blooms will sprout up all along the top of that branch.

- Top-dress with greensand and a little compost or fertilizer about once every six weeks from early fall until the end of summer. Too much fertilizing will produce a plant with all foliage and no blooms, or weak growth.

- Be patient. In three years, your roses will be wonderful. In five, they should be breathtaking.

You can buy once-blooming roses and repeat bloomers. At first, we bought mostly repeat bloomers, because they ensure that something is in bloom most of the season. However, roses that bloom once or twice a year are worth the wait, and their green, glossy foliage can be beautiful.

You can start your own roses pretty easily from cuttings. If you are patient, this is a great way to start roses. We have made cuttings from wild roses on the side of public roads and from the roses of friends. Take the rose cutting in late fall. Cut just above a five-leaf stem and plant the cutting in good soil with sand worked into it. Then pour root stimulator into the planting hole. You'll be amazed at the results!

A PRACTICUM ON WATER

Water is, of course, as vital for plants as it is for other organisms. The pressure of water within the plant cells helps the plant's leaves to remain firm. Water also is essential for most of the plant's biochemical reactions. In addition, water stores essential dissolved nutrients.

How often plants need water depends on how hot, dry, and windy the climate is, how well the plant tolerates dry conditions, and how deep the roots go into the soil. Plants can be watered at any time of day. However, to avoid plant diseases that thrive in cool, moist conditions and to reduce water loss through evaporation, most gardeners water in the early morning, when the air is cool and still, but the sun will soon dry the leaves.

The best method for watering plants is to apply the water directly to the soil, rather than over the tops of the plants. The water should be applied at a rate no faster than it can percolate into the soil, so that the excess will not run off and be wasted. This ultimately reduces water lost through evaporation and keeps leaves dry, which discourages disease.

Really, for the gardener, watering is less a chore than it is a relaxing, loving, contemplative exercise. Just set aside some quiet time at the beginning of the morning, walk among your plants, make a few mental notes of the things you want to transplant or trim up, and soak the soil thoroughly.

As with every job in the garden, watering with the right equipment makes all the difference between an enjoyable diversion and a wearisome chore. A few tools for watering the soil efficiently include hoses with tiny holes all along their surface, called soaker hoses; plastic tubes with tiny holes punched in them at intervals for drip irrigation; and plastic jugs with small holes punched in the bottom, filled with water, and set beside a plant. Watering large, densely planted areas, such as a lawn, might require some kind of sprinkler.

Evaporation of water from the soil can be minimized by covering the soil with a protective layer of good bark mulch. The mulch acts as a barrier that slows evaporation by reducing the amount of air and heat that reaches the soil surface—it can also cut down on the growth and propagation of weeds.

And remember, over-watering can be as much of a problem as under-watering. So don't overdo it.

The Formal Garden

*F*ormal gardens have essentially been attempts to recover the order, sanctity, and perfection of Paradise Lost by the competencies of man. Philosophers, architects, kings, princes, and statesmen have all turned their hands to the task at one time or another: to somehow recapture, recover, or revitalize the essence of Eden. The great gardens of Versailles and Tivoli and Belvedere and Beaudesert are part nature, part artifice; they are part humility, part hubris; they are part prose, part poesy; they are part practicum, part conundrum. Their carefully trimmed hedgerows, straight lines, proportional development, and visual architecture illumine both the many paradoxes and the great promises of gardening in this poor fallen world.

My garden does not whet the appetite; it satisfies it. It does not pro-
voke thirst through heedless indulgence, but slakes it by proffering
its natural remedy. Amid such pleasures as these have I grown old.

ⴲ EPICURUS, C. 500 B.C. ⴲ

To me, the meanest flower that ever was speaks a language that is at
once clearer, surer, and wiser than all the silvered tongues of palace
grounds. Nevertheless, there is in the formal clipped garden a sort of
solemnity, a kind of stability, a certain fortitude that bespeaks age-
lessness. We must therefore have both, the wild freedom of the blos-
som in the meadow or upon the moor and the austere ceremony and
pomp of the formal garden. Thus, may the voice of Natural
Revelation speak in both the vernacular and in the tongues of angels
higher and better than we.

ⴲ WILLIAM WORDSWORTH (1770–1850) ⴲ

I like to see flowers and herbs unfettered in the wild. But there the
beauty of the diversity and the diversity of their beauty is likely to be
swallowed up in the cacophonous spray of the whole of nature's rapture. Thus, a formal garden, like a caged bird, allows for closer
inspection, domestication, and solemn study which otherwise might
escape us altogether.

ⴲ ROBERT LOUIS STEVENSON (1850–1894) ⴲ

A formal garden is like a bud in a vase: magnificent, elegant, and somehow naturally artificial.

⊶ MARCEL PROUST (1871–1922) ⊷

Fit for kings, formal gardens afford an earthly Elysium and the odd impression that we mere men might actually control nature for a time.

⊶ EZRA POUND (1885–1972) ⊷

Time does things. It is part of your outfit. You can't control it, so you ignore it when you do things on this scale. With plants, you watch and you wait.

⊶ POLLY HILL (1907–) ⊷

Garden designing is an art form, even though it can be learned like any other subject by attending a course. Personal style is all-important. It is essential to spend time visiting gardens of various periods so you can discover how beds and borders evolve and change character over time and through the seasons. Take notes as you go; draw—even roughly— the shapes of trees and shrubs. Learn to build up your knowledge of plants, not only to be able to recognize them but to know what growing conditions they like or dislike, when they will flower, what their leaves will contribute before and after flowering, how they will relate to their neighbors. This knowledge comes only with familiarity, observation, and experience.

ᐤ ROSEMARY VEREY, C. 1994 ᐣ

This is precisely the essence of the New Formalism: we can take advantage of the many benefits offered by architectural-style gardens and then make the plan and planting as formal as we want. If you'd like a boxwood-edged garden, with fountains and borders, go ahead. . . . The important thing is not to turn away from the sense and wisdom of a historical geometric approach simply because it seems at first glance to be too stiff or rigid. In the garden you control the degree and amount of formality—you are free to pick from a wide range of related historical elements to suit your personal taste and lifestyle.

ᐤ MICHAEL WEISHAN, C. 1987 ᐣ

As is the garden, such is the gardener.

    ❧ AMERICAN PROVERB ❧

Neo-traditionalism is a form of nostalgia to be sure. But it need not be artificial or stuffy. After all, fine Shaker furniture is far more pleasing to the eye than most of the odd monstrous concoctions modern designers and manufacturers foist on their customers these days—even if the Shaker design is merely imitated for sentiment. Likewise, the recovery of the formal garden is a much more welcome trend than the heartless suburban nursery kitsch. At the very least, such imitations have historical precedents.

    ❧ E. V. RIEU (1887–1972) ❧

Consult the genius of the place in all.

    ❧ ALEXANDER POPE (1688–1774) ❧

Wild gardening sounds as attractive nowadays as a wild woman or a wild party.

    ❧ ROBIN LANE FOX, C. 1986 ❧

I have rarely seen either ruins or rivers well manufactured.

    ❧ WILLIAM GILPIN (1724–1804) ❧

What is a garden?
Goodness knows!
You've got a garden,
I suppose:
To one it is a piece of ground
For which some gravel must be found.
To some, those seeds that must be sown,
To some a lawn that must be mown.
To some, a ton of Cheddar rocks;
To some it means a window box;
To some, who dare not pick a flower,
A man, at eighteen pence an hour.
To some, it is a silly jest
About the latest garden pest;
To some, a haven where they find
Forgetfulness and peace of mind.
What is a garden
Large or small?
'Tis just a garden,
After all.

REGINALD ARKELL, C. 1935

Style is a matter of taste, design a matter of principles.
ᶿᵇ THOMAS CHURCH (1905–1978) ᶠᵉ

The blending of different elements, the subtle transition from the fixed and formal lines of art to the shifting and irregular lines of nature, and lastly in the essential convenience and liveableness of the garden, lies the fundamental secret of the old garden magic.
ᶿᵇ EDITH WHARTON (1862–1937) ᶠᵉ

Passion for display appears the ruling note in English formal horticulture of every kind and in every period: we want a show.
ᶿᵇ REGINALD FARRER (1880–1920) ᶠᵉ

Once it has a toehold, incongruity has a way of advancing systematically through the garden like quackgrass.
ᶿᵇ DESMOND KENNEDY (1945–) ᶠᵉ

All gardening is landscape painting.
ᶿᵇ HORACE WALPOLE (1717–1797) ᶠᵉ

It may seem impertinent of me to praise, but I must admire the taste Mrs. Grant has shown in all this. There is such a quiet simplicity in the plan of the walk! Not too much is attempted.
ᶿᵇ JANE AUSTEN (1775–1817) ᶠᵉ

Underlying the greatest gardens are certain principles of composition which remain unchanged because they are rooted in the natural laws of the universe.

∘{ SYLVIA CROWE, C. 1959 }∘

When smiling lawns and tasteful cottages begin to embellish the country, we know that order and culture are established.

∘{ ANDREW JACKSON DOWNING (1815–1852) }∘

Plans should be made on the ground to fit the place, and not the place made to suit some plan out of a book.

∘{ WILLIAM ROBINSON (1838–1935) }∘

You have only to think of the front gardens you drive past in the summer that are planted up almost entirely of dwarfs to realize how lacking in character and individuality they are. Such plants never get off the ground; they are mere color explosions.

∘{ CHRISTOPHER LLOYD, C. 1973 }∘

The light and the deep,
The red and the white,
Should be spaced apart.

The early and the late
Should likewise be
Planted in due order.

My desire is,
Throughout the four seasons,
To bring wine along,

And not to let
A single day pass
Without some flower opening.

                   ⊶ OU-YANG HSIU (1007–1072) ⊷

Every approach to irregularity and a wild, confused, crowded, or natural-like appearance must be avoided in gardens avowedly artificial.

ϴ JOHN CLAUDIUS LOUDON (1783–1843) ϱ

A little studied negligence is becoming in a garden, crowded, or nature.

ϴ ELEANOR PERENYI, C. 1981 ϱ

Art should never be allowed to set foot in the province of nature, otherwise than clandestinely and by night. Whenever she is allowed to appear here, and men begin to compromise the difference, night, Gothicism, confusion, and absolute chaos are come again.

ϴ WILLIAM SHENSTONE (1714–1763) ϱ

To talk of a natural or wild garden is a contradiction in terms. You might as well talk of a natural zoo, and do away with the bars, and arrange bamboo brakes for the tigers, mountaintops for the eagles, and an iceberg for the polar bears.

ϴ EDEN PHILPOTTS (1862–1960) ϱ

Subjugated gardens abound, and I can see why. Unless discipline is maintained from the moment the spirit level is laid across the earth, you are nourishing a vast, tactile, heavy scented siren which will keep you forever in its thrall.

⊶ MIRABEL OSLER, C. 1990 ⊷

He therefore who would see his flowers disposed
Slightly and in just order, ere he gives
The beds the trusted treasure of their needs
Forecasts the future whole, that when the scene
Shall break into its preconceived display,
Each for itself, and all as if with one voice
Conspiring, may attest his bright design.

⊶ WILLIAM COWPER (1731–1800) ⊷

It is unchristian to hedge from the sight of others the beauties of nature which it has been our good fortune to create or secure.

⊶ FRANK SCOTT (1828–1919) ⊷

CHEEK AND FLEMING'S CHEEKWOOD

The changing seasons were what did it. Every season so distinct, with its own charms and attractions. Mabel Wood Cheek had been raised in nearby Clarksville, and she loved the natural beauty of Middle Tennessee. Far enough south to experience lingering springtimes and autumns, with warm days and cool evenings far into the summertime, yet far enough north to escape the extreme temperatures of the Deep South. The Cumberland Plateau gave Nashville enough elevation to experience cooler temperatures and hilly vistas, yet just minutes to the north, in Kentucky, snowfalls were much deeper, winters were much longer, and temperatures were much lower.

Middle Tennessee seemed just right to Mrs. Cheek, surveying the view from Cheek Mansion just south of downtown Nashville. Her husband Leslie had traveled all over Europe, along with architect Bryant Fleming, so that Leslie could make informed choices about architecture and landscaping for the one-hundred-acre property and mansion to be built on it.

Completed in 1933, Cheekwood was a showpiece of Georgian Revival architecture, fitted right into the landscape as if it arose from the limestone on which it was built. Fleming used the limestone to his advantage as he designed the gardens surrounding the mansion: formal close to the house, with less formality as the land dropped away from the home.

Leslie Cheek's love for boxwood became an obsession. He traveled throughout the South, collecting mature boxwoods, along with their stories of origin, to plant at Cheekwood. The stories have long disappeared, but the boxwood gardens themselves have been restored to their original formal design.

Mr. Cheek died just three years after Cheekwood was completed. Mabel Cheek lived on in the house for fourteen years of changing seasons, until she gave the home to her daughter and son-in-law Hulda and Walter Sharp. The Sharps sold off some of the perimeter acreage, taking the land down to a more manageable fifty-five acres. Realizing the worth of the property as a trophy of southern heritage and values, in 1955 the Sharps gave Cheekwood and all her property to a nonprofit organization, working with the Exchange Club and what is now known as the Horticultural Society of Middle Tennessee. Members of the Horticultural Society worked endless hours weeding, restoring, and reclaiming the gardens to their original intent and beauty, and in 1960 Cheekwood Gardens opened to the public, a perpetual gift to Nashville, middle Tennessee, and visitors from around the world.

The Sharps moved to a part of the property known as Owl's Hill, which they later gave to Cheekwood to form the Owl's Hill Nature Center. Mrs. Sharp died in 2000.

Recently a gift of seventeen million dollars combined with other gifts to fund a multiyear, $18 million–plus renovation and expansion.

Master landscape architect Michael Van Faulkenberg has overseen the renovations to Bryant Fleming's original gardens, as well as the addition of new ones, such as the seasons garden Van Faulkenberg designed himself, and the color garden, blooming with flowers changed out every spring, summer, and fall, designed by landscape architect Naud Burnett.

Other specialty gardens include the Japanese garden, the herb garden, two perennial gardens, water gardens, and the award-winning wildflower garden. Pools, fountains, statuary, the extensive boxwood plantings, and awesome views of the tumbling hills of Tennessee combine with the beautiful gardens to make Cheekwood a precious treasure.

Cheekwood has expanded its collections over the years as well. Current collections include the camellia, daffodil, daylily, iris, orchid, rose, and trillium collections, and an unusual cloud forest filled with plants from Panama.

In addition, the Cheek mansion hosts changing series of important art collections.

The formal garden is a hybrid garden, with characteristics of both public park and home gardens. While most of us will never have the opportunity to develop gardens as extensive as those at Cheekwood, elements of the formal garden may be included in any well-planned garden.

The key to a formal garden, regardless of size, is proper planning.

Just as the Cheek property reflects its character through the use of native building materials and repetitive use of these same materials in the gardens, any homeowner can enter into a relationship with a local landscape architect to prevent costly mistakes as well as include important elements of design into an overall plan to follow through years of planting and maintaining. This relationship is like any other: shared by two parties with similar tastes and goals. Any experienced gardener can purchase design books at the nearby nursery or home improvement shop. Unfortunately, this seems to be the extent of training of many who purport to be landscape architects. Ask anyone you are thinking of hiring important questions: Do they have photographs of properties for which they have designed plantings? Do they try to include native plants? How do they wed plant design with the structure of the home?

There is little inspiration in the typical subdivision developer's standard plan of three holly bushes with a tall tree on one corner and some short bushy grass in the front of the bed along the sidewalk. Sometimes, someone will get creative and add a wavy line with a bench or "garden feature" to spice things up. Don't invest in a design book if this is all you can really keep up with. For $4.95, you can copy a planting from a magazine, or order a complete bed from a mail-order company—order their shade garden, water garden, or four seasons garden.

However, if you are going to spend hundreds or thousands of

dollars on a landscape architect, make certain to see his or her work in person. Visit some former work sites. See if the plantings "fit" the house. In the summer, are sprinklers constantly whirring? Has any native stone or wood been incorporated into the design? Are there any paths, and if so, do they reflect the feeling of the neighborhood, and from what you can tell, the owners' tastes?

Some of this may not even be important to you. There are many people who hire interior decorators to implant good design into a home, but the home doesn't reflect anything of its inhabitants except their insecure desire to impress others. It is easy to pick these homes out by the unread antiquarian books artfully displayed alongside the unusual and unusually expensive artwork. If you can think of your garden as a room, and in this case a formal room, how would it reflect *you* as well as follow basic elements of formal design?

Some of the most interesting formal gardens are simply hedges, such as Cheekwood's boxwood garden. Think of the time some sorts of hedges take to keep them well groomed. Others can go without clipping for longer periods of time.

Do you want your garden to be a seasonal showcase, or consist mainly of bushes and trees, the backbones of any garden?

Even in the smallest yard, you can import elements of formal design if that's your bent. Just keep scale in mind. Everything from concrete goose statues to Italian garden structures in small scale can be found these days.

To plan your own formal garden, visit local formal gardens in your area. See what native plants and focal points (fountains, pools, statuary, hedges) are incorporated into the design. Keep in mind that you can't use every idea; your garden features must remain in scale with your home and the size of your property.

Taunton's magazine has wonderful design tips that are classic and timeless. Check out books on formal gardens from your local library and fill your mind with good design.

Steal ideas relentlessly from the gardens in your area that you love. Imitation is the greatest form of flattery!

A Practicum on Legacies

We moderns tend to be enamored of progress. We live at a time when things shiny and new are prized far above things old and time-worn. For most of us, traditions and legacies are little more than the gewgaws of quirky and nostalgic sentimentalism. They are hardly more than the dronings and monotonous successions of obsolete notions, anachronous ideals, and antiquarian habits—sound and fury signifying nothing. But many of the wisest of men and women through the ages have recognized that tradition is a foundation upon which all true advancement must be built—that it is, in fact, the prerequisite to all genuine progress.

Winston Churchill argued, "The greatest advances in human

civilization have come when we recovered what we had lost: when we learned the lessons of history." Likewise, Woodrow Wilson asserted, "A nation which does not remember what it was yesterday, does not know what it is today, nor what it is trying to do. We are trying to do a futile thing if we do not know where we came from or what we have been about. Ours is a rich legacy. Rich but lost."

In the midst of such whirling change, we sometimes need to be reminded of the efficacy of tradition to offer stability, continuity, and guidance. We need to reinforce the notion that connections to the past are the only sure leads to the future.

What is true of nations and cultures is equally true of gardens. But while with nations and cultures resorting to traditions and legacies necessitates long hours in the library and the recovery of long-abandoned worldviews, in the garden it involves little more than the passing on of the practical joys of working the soil, cutting and pruning, planting and transplanting, weeding and watering. In other words, we can pass on our gardening legacies in the unhurried context of relationships, conversations, and shared labors.

Stable societies must be eternally vigilant in the task of handing on their great legacies—to remember and then to inculcate that remembrance in the hearts and minds of their children. The venerable aphorism, "He who forgets his own history is condemned to repeat it," ought to be the credo of every passing generation. After all, any people who do not know their own history will simply have to endure all the same mistakes, sacrifices, and absurdities of the past all over again.

Sadly, such realizations are very nearly lost on us in this odd to-whom-it-may-concern, instant-everything day of microwavable meals, prefab buildings, bottom-rung bureaucracy, fit-for-the-market education, knee-jerk public misinformation, and predigested formula entertainment. Thus, temporary expediencies supersede permanent exigencies.

Gardening is a wonderful reminder to slow down, to make every moment matter, to work hard toward a good end, to defer gratification for a time, and to be patient knowing that in the end the doings of God are but in the hands of God.

Those are important lessons—lessons that can be learned and then passed on as legacies from one generation to the next. The great English lexographer and wit Samuel Johnson said, "A contempt of the monuments and the wisdom of the past, may be justly reckoned one of the reigning follies of these days, to which pride and idleness have equally contributed." He might well have had gardening in mind when he said that.

The Working Garden

Nearly every serious gardener considers their little plot a working garden—a place where experiments are undertaken, new strains are tested, new tricks are tried, new methods are attempted, and new ideas are given full throttle. It is part of the joy of the garden graces to see what will and what will not work. This is the grand tradition that one veteran gardener passes on to the neophyte. It is the remarkable legacy of something that is clearly far more an art than a science.

I must observe that neither the number of the fine arts nor the particular arts entitled to that appellation have been fixed by general consent. Many reckon but five: Painting, sculpture, architecture, music and poetry. To these some have added Oratory, including within that Rhetoric which is the art of style and composition. Others again, add Gardening as a seventh fine art. Not horticulture, but the art of embellishing grounds by fancy.

of THOMAS JEFFERSON (1743–1826) po

I've noticed something about gardening. You set out to do one thing and pretty soon you're doing something else, which leads to some other thing, and so on. By the end of the day, you look at the shovel stuck in the half dug rose bed and wonder what on earth you've been doing.

of ANNE RAVER (1949–) po

What a man needs in gardening is a cast-iron back, with a hinge in it.

     ◆{ CHARLES DUDLEY WARNER (1829–1900) }◆

The circumstances of gardeners, generally mean, and always moderate, may satisfy us that their great ingenuity is not commonly over-recompensed. Their delightful art is practiced by so many rich people for amusement, that little advantage is to be made by those who practice it for profit.

     ◆{ ADAM SMITH (1723–1790) }◆

O stagnant east wind, palsied mare,
Giddap! The ruby roses' hair
Must blow.

Behold how order is the end
Of everything. The roses bend
As one.

Order, the law of hoes and rakes,
May be perceived in windy quakes
And squalls.

The gardener searches earth and sky
The truth in nature to espy
In vain.

He well might find that eager balm
In lilies' stately-statued calm;
But then

He well might find it in this fret
Of lilies rusted, rotting, wet
With rain.

           WALLACE STEVENS (1879–1955)

Don't wear perfume in the garden—unless you want to be pollinated
by bees.

                                ANNE RAVER (1949–)

Those who labor in the earth are the chosen people of God, if He
ever had a chosen people.

                          THOMAS JEFFERSON (1743–1826)

Gardeners have three weapons to use against summer drought:
mulches, watering pots, and prayers.

                           TYLER WHITTLE (1927–1994)

Oh, Adam was a gardener, and God who made him sees
That half the proper gardener's work is done upon his knees
So, when your work is finished, you can wash your hands and pray
For the glory of the Garden that it may not pass away.

                       RUDYARD KIPLING (1865–1936)

Gardening reality is born with a hoe in the hand.

                           SARA STEIN, C. 1988

Having commenced gardening, I study the arts of pruning, sowing, and planting; and enterprise everything in that way, from melons down to cabbages. I have a large garden to display my abilityes in; and were we twenty miles nearer London I might turn higgler, and serve your honor with cauliflowers and broccoli at the best hand.

❧ WILLIAM COWPER (1731–1800) ❧

By dint of hard work, constant care, and endless buckets of water, he had even become a creator, inventing certain tulips and dahlias which seemed to have been forgotten by nature.

❧ VICTOR HUGO (1802–1885) ❧

What do gardeners do in the winter? They accumulate fat.

❧ GEOFFREY CHARLESWORTH, C. 1988 ❧

But though an old man, I am but a young gardener.
        ◦⊦ THOMAS JEFFERSON (1743–1826) ⊦◦

The garden that is finished is dead.
        ◦⊦ H. E. BATES (1905–1974) ⊦◦

No sentiment is more acknowledged in the family of Agriculturists than the few who can afford it should incur the risk and expense of all new improvements, and give the benefit freely to the many of more restricted circumstances.
        ◦⊦ THOMAS JEFFERSON (1743–1826) ⊦◦

JEFFERSON'S MONTICELLO

The tall farmer strode purposefully down the steps toward the garden. The day had been frustrating, with pressing indoor work claiming most of the precious daylight hours. It was May, and though there was more daylight now than during the cold, wet winter months, days were always too short for Thomas Jefferson. Each task that day was motivated by the promise to himself that he would soon be released from his office to inspect the progress of the vegetable garden. Each finished task had been followed by the receipt of an important letter, a visitor, or an overseer needing personal instructions. Late visitors complained under their breath at his brevity and severe countenance. How could he tell them he preferred the company of damp black soil and new green leaves to their own? His fine manners failed to belie the impatient tapping of his toe or the frequent glances reviewing the progress of the sun. Finally he was alone, the last papers, guests, and workmen dealt with. He tugged on his work boots, not bothering to take the time to change into old clothing.

Jefferson negotiated the steps down into the vegetable garden, but did not check his pace until he arrived at the pea patch. He had planted three varieties of peas this year, in soil enriched with plenty of manure. The manure for this bed came from the horses that had been fed pumpkins all winter long. Those pumpkins had been manured the summer before and had performed exceedingly well, providing feed not only for the horses, but also the hogs. It was an experiment Jefferson was in the midst of: comparing the results and price of pumpkins and feed corn for some of his animals. Long before the term "organic gardening" entered the common vernacular, Jefferson innately knew that a good farmer relies on soil amendments and healthy plants as the best means to discourage insect invasions and crop disease. He understood the connection between good soil, intentionally careful animal husbandry, and good plant stock.

The president looked at the healthy strong stems of the green peas and searched among the creamy white blooms for a pod. It was possible that the first peas had already been picked this morning and that they were being prepared even now for a suppertime surprise. His fingers searched among the stems as he tried to distinguish a plump pod from among the flat, immature ones in the waning twilight. He twisted his head upward when he heard warblers headed down to the orchard, but his fingers never stopped exploring the matted vines. Aha! He plucked a fat pod from the middle of a row on the inside, down low. He held the green pod up to the sunlight and appreciated its size, its shape, and the moistness of the skin. This variety, from Leitch's store in Charlottesville, was producing well in the Virginia climate. The southeastern vantage of the garden plot and the excellent sloping drainage conspired to give every variety of fruit or vegetable planted the optimum chance for success.

Mr. Jefferson used his ink-stained thumbnail to open the plump pod, removed one pea, and popped it into his mouth. He closed his eyes and laughed aloud at the slight crunch and burst of flavor. For all the fancy French cuisine he'd tasted, served on all the gold-trimmed china, and in the brightest company, he would still choose this: the first pea from between his own thumb and finger in the company of his own land.

Called the "Bloodless Revolution of 1800," Thomas Jefferson's election marked a profound but peaceful change in the administration of the young American nation. The revolutionist who boldly wrote religious and ethical beliefs into the Declaration of Independence brought to the presidency a philosophy of government firmly rooted in those same beliefs, a philosophy that concerned itself, above all, with the rights and liberties of the individual. It was Jefferson's democratic views, with his enduring faith in the individual, that, more than anything else, turned the country away from the class rule of the Federalists.

Few men have been better equipped to become president—a graduate of William and Mary College and an able lawyer, Jefferson helped shape the destiny of the struggling nation from the beginning. He served in the Virginia House of Burgesses; in the Continental Congress—where he wrote the final draft of the Declaration; as a minister in the French court; as governor of Virginia; as secretary of state under Washington; and vice president under Adams. But as president, Jefferson proved that philosophic ability and experience in office were no replacements for political leadership. He was a remarkable inventor, a scientist, a writer, an artist, a planter, an architect, a musician, and an educator—but he was a poor politician and administrator. Instead, he ever and always remained a farmer at heart. Writing to Charles Willson Peale in 1811, he admitted, "I have often thought that if heaven had given me choice of my position and calling, it should have been on a rich spot of earth, well watered, and near a good market for the productions of the garden. No occupation is so delightful to me as the culture of the earth, and no culture comparable to that of the garden. Such a variety of subjects, some one always coming to perfection, the failure of one thing repaired by the success of another, and instead of one harvest a continued one through the year. Under a total want of demand except for our family table, I am still devoted to the garden. But though an old man, I am but a young gardener."

As president he was able, however, to bring a profound sense of democracy to the nation's capital, an accomplishment that ranks with the celebrated purchase of the Louisiana Territory as an outstanding achievement of his administration. A complex, brilliant man, Jefferson was one of the most accomplished of our presidents—he was talented as are few men in any age—the living example of his own abiding belief in the capacity of the individual to learn and to grow under freedom.

Nevertheless, his heart was always with the soil—and particularly the working soil of his home at Monticello.

This reality was dramatically highlighted during his term as vice president under John Adams. He traveled to Baltimore on official business and asked for a room in the city's best hotel. Not recognizing the great man—who always traveled dressed in modest working clothes and without a retinue of servants—the proprietor turned him away.

Soon after Jefferson's departure, the innkeeper was informed that he had just sent away the author of the Declaration of Independence and hero of the Revolutionary War. Horrified, he promptly dispatched a number of his employees to find the vice president and offer him as many rooms as he required. Jefferson, who had already taken a room at another hotel, was not at all flattered or amused. He sent the man who found him back with the message, "Tell the innkeeper that I value his good intentions highly, but if he has no room for a dirty farmer, he shall have none for the vice president."

It was not merely the spirit of democratic solidarity or of judicial propriety that piqued Jefferson's ire in that situation. He had always prided himself on being a man of the soil first and foremost. He was America's preeminent agrarian theorist. He was an avid gardener and a skilled botanist. His gardening journals have inspired generations of farmers and planters. And his agricultural innovations helped to make American harvests the envy of the world.

He strongly believed that an attachment to the land was the chief mark of an advanced culture. He believed that the fate of a nation was ultimately decided by the attitude of that nation to its soil. He said, "Widespread distribution and careful stewardship over property is the most tangible attribute of liberty. The faith of a people, the vision of a people, the destiny of a people may be divined by its corporate concern for the soil."

Jefferson's granddaughter, Ellen Randolph Coolidge, described this Founding Father as a gardener first and foremost: "He loved farming and gardening, the fields, the orchards, and his asparagus beds. Every day he rode through his plantation and walked in his garden. In the cultivation of the last he took great pleasure. Of flowers, too, he was very fond. One of my early recollections is of the attention which he paid to his flower-beds. He kept up a correspondence with persons in the large cities, for the purpose of receiving supplies of roots and seeds both for his kitchen and flower garden. I remember well when he first returned to Monticello, how immediately he began to prepare new beds for his flowers. I remember the planting of the first hyacinths and tulips, and their subsequent growth. The roots arrived, labeled each one with a fancy name. There was Marcus Aurelius, and the King of the Gold Mine, the Roman Empress, and the Queen of the Amazons, Psyche, the God of Love, etc., etc., etc. . . . Then when the flowers were in bloom, and we were in ecstasies over the rich purple and crimson, or pure white, or delicate lilac, or pale yellow of the blossoms, how he would sympathize in our admiration, or discuss with my mother and elder sister new groupings and combinations and contrasts. Oh, these were happy moments for us and for him."

His all too infrequent and temporary stints at home between his official duties in Washington would find him engaging in his heart's desire, the pursuit of agriculture. His public service exposed him to a wider world and imposed upon his farmer's blood the desire to develop more and ever more plant varieties to improve American life and economy, developing the horticultural gardener's characteristic curiosity, scientific persuasion, and generosity.

His inherited plantation holdings of Shadwell, Monticello, Poplar Forest, Tomahawk, and Bear Creek were so vast that he had experience with several types of soil and climate conditions, and they became his laboratories both individually and for the collective betterment of an emerging nation with the development of new agricultural tools and laborsaving devices. His attention to methods of cultivation and crop rotation to combat soil erosion and depletion were so ahead of his time as to be breathtaking.

Jefferson grew vegetable, fruit, and fiber crops, as well as tobacco, always trying out new varieties. He motivated the formation of agricultural societies to facilitate the sharing of successful farming techniques. When the house at Shadwell burned down along with most of his extensive library, he moved to Monticello, which he used as the main experimental base for new seed and plant varieties. He exchanged agricultural correspondence with George Washington, among others. The two famous men complained to one another often about the reluctance of their farm overseers to support their attempts at modernization and crop experimentation. When they would of necessity leave their plantations to serve their country in public office, their overseers would often wreak havoc on their careful plans for scientific progress.

In 1795, George Washington, another gardening Founding Father, wrote to Jefferson of their mutual interests: "This, like all other things of the sort with me, since my absence from home, have come to nothing; for neither my Overseers nor Manager, will attend properly to anything but the crops they have usually cultivated: and in spite of all I can say, if there is the smallest discretionary power allowed them, they will fill the land with Indian corn; although they have demonstrable proof, at every step they take, of its destructive effects. I am resolved however, as soon as it shall be in my power to attend a little more closely to my own concerns, to make this crop yield, in a great degree to other grain; to pulses, and to grasses. I am beginning again with Chicory from a handful of seed given me by Mr. Stricklan."

Jefferson kept up a lively plant exchange with friends the world over, a rewarding yet frustrating experience given the hazardous methods of transportation in his day. Shipments were often lost at sea or would freeze and be ruined when making their way over land. In Jefferson's *Farm Book* as well as his *Garden Book*, letter after letter laments the loss of a full horticultural shipment: "Until the last autumn, I have every autumn written to Madame de Tessé and sent her a box of seeds. I saw with infinite mortification that they were either carried into England or arrived so late as to answer no purpose to her. The state of the ocean the last fall was, and continues to be, so desperate that it is vain to attempt anything again till that can be changed." Jefferson to Marquis de Lafayette, 1808: "There was lately shipped for me from Philadelphia one box of grape vines, and four open boxes of monthly strawberries from Italy. Although from the account I receive of the latter they seem irrecoverable yet if there be any hope of life I would ask the favor of you to give them to any careful gardener in Richmond who will hereafter furnish me with some roots from them if they live. Their value is great, as in our climate they should bear nine months in the year."

Jefferson also utilized his opportunities for extensive overseas travel to enlarge his understanding of horticulture when he was "resting" from diplomatic pursuits. In February of 1786 John Adams summoned Jefferson to London to help negotiate a treaty with Portugal, among other obligations. Jefferson complied, but also used any available free time during his visit to compile copious notes from tours of English gardens. Like any serious gardener, he obviously desired to learn from the great masters of gardening so that his own holdings could reflect gardening heritage well executed. Even reading just one of his entries, it is obvious that he had a scientific eye for detail and an aesthetic eye for probity: "Esher-Place: The house in a bottom near the river; on the other side the ground rises pretty much. The road by which we come to the house forms a dividing line in the middle of the front; on the right are heights, rising one beyond and above another, with clumps of trees; on the farthest a temple. A hollow filled up with a clump of trees, the tallest in the bottom, so that the top is quite flat. On the left the ground descends. Clumps of trees, the clumps on each hand balance finely—a most lovely mixture of concave and convex. The garden is of about forty-five acres, besides the park which joins. Belongs to Lady Frances Pelham."

Viewed through a contemporary lens, Jefferson's use of slave labor to accomplish his lifetime horticultural goals neutralizes their great import. His was the mind, the wisdom, and the financing for effecting great arboricultural progress and diversity within an emerging nation—but the nation was based in individual freedom, and there lies the most contradictory rub. In his defense, he worked for the emancipation of slaves from the time of his induction into the Virginia state legislature. In 1814 he wrote to Mr. Edward Coles, "From an early stage of our revolution other and more distant duties were assigned to me, so that from that time till my return from Europe in 1789, and I may say till I returned to reside at home in

1809, I had little opportunity of knowing the progress of public sentiment here on this subject. I had always hoped that the younger generation, receiving their early impressions after the flame of liberty had been kindled in every breast, and had become as it were the vital spirit of every American, that the generous temperament of youth, analogous to the motion of their blood, and above the suggestions of avarice, would have sympathized with oppression where ever found, and proved their love of liberty beyond their own share of it. But intercourse with them, since my return, has not been sufficient to ascertain that they had made towards this point the progress I had hoped. Your solitary but welcome voice is the first which has brought this sound to my ear, and I have considered the general silence which prevails on this subject as indicating an apathy unfavorable to every hope. Yet the hour of emancipation is advancing in the march of time. It will come; and whether brought on by the generous energy of our minds, or by the bloody process of St. Domingo, it is a leaf of our history not yet turned over."

Suffice it to say that whatever our personal opinions on judging figures outside of their time frame, much credit must be given to the Jeffersonian slaves on whose backs lay the cultivation of his land.

The great farmer was forever grafting grapevines, introducing olive trees from Spain to friends in more southern states, and planting nut trees across the continent. With an aesthete's view of beauty, a lawyer's logic, a scientist's knowledge of specie and genus, and a farmer's soul, Jefferson embodied the early American Founding Father: his heart belonged at home, but his public life was ever devoted to his nation. And we all are the better for it.

A Practicum on Soil

Good, rich, healthy soil is indispensable for a fruitful garden. Plants derive water, oxygen for their roots, and essential nutrients from the soil. Thus, much of the work of gardening is the work of building up and maintaining the soil.

All soil consists of two basic components: minerals from weathered rocks and organic matter from decayed organisms and animal wastes. The mineral content of the soil provides plants with their essential nutrients, such as calcium, potassium, and phosphorus. Organic matter improves drainage and helps prevent waterlogged soil, reducing the occurrence of diseases such as root rot. It also binds the mineral nutrients so they remain in the soil and are not washed away. The spaces, or pores, between the tiny particles of minerals and organic matter are occupied by either water or air. Water holds vital dissolved nutrients, while air provides the roots with oxygen. Most plants do best in a soil in which about half the pore space is filled with air and the other half with moisture.

Plants use nutrients obtained from soil to build the cells and tissues needed for growth and maturation. Nutrients that plants need in large amounts, called macronutrients, include oxygen, hydrogen, carbon, and an array of minerals. They also need micronutrients, or trace elements, which consist of such things as cobalt, chlorine, boron, iron, zinc, molybdenum, nickel, manganese, and copper.

Soil texture, the size of the individual soil particles, affects how fast water drains and how well plants absorb nutrients. The largest soil particles are grains of sand. Sand grains fit loosely together with large gaps between them, resembling marbles in a jar. The large pores let water—as well as the nutrients contained in it— drain out too quickly for most plants to absorb it. Clay particles, on the other hand, are very tiny, and they pack closely together, resembling tiny beads in a jar. The pores between clay particles are so small that water drains through them very slowly. Slow drainage can lead to oxygen deprivation because the water takes the place of air in the pores. Another disadvantage of clay is that it binds water and some nutrients so tightly that most plants cannot absorb them. A third soil particle is silt, which is larger than clay but smaller than sand.

Most garden plants and herbs thrive in a soil type known as loam, which consists of roughly 50 percent sand, 25 percent clay, and 25 percent silt. A loam soil drains water well, but not too quickly, and as a result, the plant can absorb nutrients more readily. Exceptions include desert plants, such as cacti, which do best in a sandy soil, and cottonwoods, which flourish in silty soils.

In practical terms what this means is that you will likely have to spend a great deal of your gardening efforts balancing or augmenting the soil of your little plot. You'll have to break it up, turn it over, and add mulch, silt, sand, or loam. You may also have to test the soil's acidity or alkalinity. Most plants absorb nutrients best in a soil with a pH between 6.5 and 7.5. But of course that varies from specimen to specimen—plants such as rhododendrons require an acidic soil, while others, such as lilacs, grow better in an alkaline soil. Acidic soils are more common in the eastern half of the United States, where rainfall is plentiful, while alkaline soils are more common in the drier West.

Some gardeners attempt to augment their soil's richness with fertilizers—because their garden plot either does not have enough nutrients or does not have the right balance of nutrients. In addition, plants remove nutrients from the soil as they grow, so these nutrients must be replaced in order for the soil to remain productive.

Virtually all fertilizers are divided into two categories: synthetic and organic. Synthetic fertilizers are concentrated salts or minerals, some of which are produced as byproducts of petroleum production. Organic fertilizers originate in plants, animals, or minerals, and include compost, seaweed, and ground bone. Because we are organic gardeners and do not desire to use any more chemicals in our lives than we already have to by virtue of living in the twenty-first century, we never use synthetic fertilizers.

Amazingly, there are hundreds, perhaps even thousands, of ways to augment the fertility of soil without having to resort to chemicals that may pollute the water table, poison animals, or create an imbalance in the small ecosystem around the garden. The resources for organic gardeners are abundant, and approaching the soil in a more natural fashion actually only enhances the experience of the gardening graces. We think Jefferson would have heartily approved.

The Meditation Garden

Gardens are invariably quiet and serene. They are havens where we can think. They are refuges from the helter-skelter of our daily grinds. They are sanctuaries where we can pray, reflect, and ponder. Throughout history some of the greatest advances, some of the keenest insights, and some of the most creative efforts were born in meditative moments walking in gardens. Hardly just ornamentation for homes or churches or public places, gardens have always provided space for bodies and souls to explore the frontiers of truth and freedom.

Flowers reflect the human search for meaning. Does not each of us, no matter how our life has gone, ache to have a life as beautiful and true to itself as that of a flower?

            ❧ PHILLIP MOFFITT, C. 1951 ❧

Flowers are not flowers unto the poet's eyes,
Their beauty thrills him with an inward sense;
He knows that outward seemings are but lies,
Or, at the most, but earthly shadows, whence
The soul that looks within for truth may guess
The presence of some wondrous heavenliness.

            ❧ JAMES RUSSELL LOWELL (1819–1891) ❧

I always think of my sins when I weed. They grow apace in the same way and are harder still to get rid of.

            ❧ HELENA RUTHERFORD ELY (1858–1920) ❧

How fair is a garden amid the trials and passions of existence.

            ❧ BENJAMIN DISRAELI (1804–1881) ❧

Indeed, it is the purest of human pleasures. It is the greatest refreshment to the spirit of man; without which buildings and palaces are but gross handy works: and a man shall ever see that when ages grow to civility and elegance, men come to build stately, sooner then to garden finely: as if gardening were the greater perfection.

ᛞ FRANCIS BACON (1561–1626) ᛞ

It seems to me far from an exaggeration that good professors are not more essential to a college, than a spacious garden, which ought to be formed with the nicest elegance, tempered with simplicity, rejecting sumptuous and glaring ornaments.

ᛞ LORD HENRY HOME (1696–1782) ᛞ

The kiss of the sun for pardon,
The song of the birds for mirth,
One is nearer God's heart in the garden
Than anywhere else on earth.

ᛞ DOROTHY FRANCES GURNEY (1858–1932) ᛞ

When in these fresh mornings I go into my garden before anyone is awake, I go for the time being into perfect happiness. In this hour divinely fresh and still, the fair face of every flower salutes me with a silent joy that fills me with infinite content; each gives me its color, its grace, its perfume, and enriches me with the consummation of its beauty.

CELIA THAXTER (1835–1894)

Gardening is an outlet for fanaticism, violence, love, and rationality without any of their worst side effects.

GEOFFREY CHARLESWORTH, C. 1994

The garden is frightful! It drips, it listens:
Is the rain in loneliness here,
Squeezing a branch like lace at a window,
Or is there a witness near?

The earth is heavy with swollen burdens;
Smothered, the spongy weald.
Listen! Afar, as though it were August,
Night ripens in a field.

No sound. Not a stranger around to spy
The night. In the garden alone,
Rain starts up again, dripping and tumbling
On roof, gutter, flagstone.

I'll bring the rain to my lips, and listen:
Am I in loneliness here,
In the rain, bursting with tears, in darkness,
Or is there a witness near?

Deep silence. Not even a leaf is astir.
No gleam of light to be seen.
Only choking sobs and the splash of his slippers,
And his sighs and tears between.

    ◅ BORIS PASTERNAK (1890–1960) ▻

The force through the green fuse drives the flower,
Drives my green age.
> ⊶ DYLAN THOMAS (1914–1953) ⊷

I had not the smallest taste for growing plants, or taking care of them. My whole time passed in staring at them, or into them. In no morbid curiosity, but in admiring wonder.
> ⊶ JOHN RUSKIN (1819–1900) ⊷

Who would dangerously look up at planets that might safely look down at plants?
> ⊶ JOHN GERARD (1545–1612) ⊷

Half the interest of the garden is the constant exercise of the imagination.
> ⊶ MRS. C. W. EARLE (1836–1925) ⊷

There is not a sprig of grass that shoots uninteresting to me.
⊶ THOMAS JEFFERSON (1743–1826) ⊷

'Tis my faith that every flower
Enjoys the air it breathes!
⊶ WILLIAM WORDSWORTH (1770–1850) ⊷

I don't know how people deal with their moods when they have no garden, raspberry patch or field to work in. You can take your angers, frustrations, bewilderments to the earth, working savagely, working up a sweat and an ache and a great weariness. The work rinses out the cup of your spirit, leaves it washed and clean and ready to be freshly filled with new hope.
⊶ RACHEL PEDEN, C. 1970 ⊷

Many gardeners will agree that hand-weeding is not the terrible drudgery that it is often made out to be. Some people find in it a kind of soothing monotony. It leaves their minds free to develop the plot for their next novel or to perfect the brilliant repartee with which they should have encountered a relative's latest example of unreasonableness.
⊶ CHRISTOPHER LLOYD, C. 1973 ⊷

We ought to spend more time, I think, opening our heart to the beauty of the world, especially in May. Just looking and feeling and smelling the brave sweet fragrances of spring. Of them all, the lilac is the loveliest. There is enough beauty in a lilac for a lifetime. The shape of every tiny flower is delicate, and the whole cluster a pointed spear of exquisite loveliness. Then the leaves themselves are wonderful, polished and dark and smooth in texture. And then there is the dark, cool fragrance to enchant the senses.

ᡒ GLADYS TABER (1899–1980) ᡒ

Flowers have a mysterious and subtle influence upon the feelings, not unlike some strains of music. They relax the tenseness of the mind. They dissolve its rigor.

ᡒ HENRY WARD BEECHER (1813–1877) ᡒ

Brother Cadfael's Shrewsbury

She walked through the garden slowly, pausing when exquisite scents penetrated her grief. Something about the pungent scent of rosemary waked her up to the loveliness around her. Another wave of sadness gripped her heart in that tight, constricting way. Tears stung her eyes, and she wondered if she would ever feel better. Immediately, guilt crept in, ugly, crouching, not quite in view, but hunched down low in a corner of her mind. How could she think about her own feelings, when he was dead, never to feel again. How petty to concentrate on feelings, when any feeling at all was a gift.

Confused, she continued, the gravel path crunching beneath her feet. This rose, "Penelope," this beautiful apricot-pink rose, bloomed profusely, crawling all over the trellis it was trained on, yet leaping over to the very eaves of the building. She couldn't resist smelling its fragrance. Pulling a rose near her nose, she strained to get closer while avoiding the sharp thorns of the vine it grew on. Oh! Another lesson. The thorns that seem to come with so many sweetnesses in life. What was that C. S. Lewis quote again? Ah, yes, "To love at all is to be vulnerable. Love anything, and your heart will certainly be wrung and possibly be broken. If you want to make sure of keeping it intact, you must give your heart to no one. . . . It will not be broken; it will become unbreakable, impenetrable, irredeemable. The alternative to tragedy, or at least to the risk of tragedy, is damnation. The only place outside of heaven where you can be perfectly safe from all the dangers and perturbations of love is Hell."

Yes, she had loved, and she still loved, but the love was no longer returned, except in memory. All the pain of that loss came as another wave of grief hit her. She inhaled the scent of the rose deeply, and the pleasure of its smell intermingled with sorrow until the sorrow had a sweetness to it, impossible to describe.

Every plant taught a lesson. "God shouts in pain," C. S. Lewis, again. Weeds grew quickly, weak plants struggled for life and always required attention. Some plants appeared to thrive, yet their roots were weak, and they died with little notice. Others struggled against all odds—drought, insect damage, poor soil—and valiantly bloomed despite the constant battles. The lamb's ears felt soft as she rubbed them against her cheek and between her fingers.

She paused at the end of the path, before leaving the garden. She surveyed the colors of the flowers in bloom, and the differences in the foliage. She took in the sight of butterflies and birds flitting about within the garden. She noted where the beautiful bulbs of spring had been, now resting silently beneath the soil. They would come back next spring. She breathed deeply and caught the scent of the soil—fresh, earthy, damp, alive. She exited the garden, closing the gate slowly behind her. Still sorrowful, she was now calm in her spirit, soothed by creation's balm, for now.

Gardens are a gift to people in pain. The ability to get out to a garden, to enter into a peaceful sanctuary, is a tremendous help to the hurting. It is ministry to the soul when the hurting one can see beauty with the eyes, smell loveliness to heal the spirit's raw places, hear birdsong and the breeze among leaves and seed heads rattling. Touching a leaf and rubbing it reminds us of life, of diversity of experience, of intricacy and individuality in design.

The day comes when the gardener can participate with the garden again. Getting down on knees, she can pull up a weed, pat the earth around a new plant, pour water on dry, parched earth that has been ignored for a while. It is a welcome distraction. It seems simultaneously petty and very, very important. This confusion mirrors her own internal confusion. Placing the trowel deep into the earth and uprooting the dead flowers, cutting back the old bee balm, trimming the dying iris leaves, watering the neglected roses, which refuse to bloom without water, she is rewarded one day as the garden begins to bloom again. It is a messenger of hope, and she needs messengers of hope right now who speak softly, gently, and with few words and much profundity.

This would be a good spot for a memorial garden. What would a garden representing him be like? No, not off in the woods alone. He never liked being alone very much. More sociable than herself, she thought with a smile. He wasn't much for the pastel colors that she liked, either. When left to his own choices, he liked bright reds, blues, yellows. She cocked her head to one side. His garden would have to be in the middle of things, with bright flowers. It needed two or three things in it. Something with words, to reflect his deep faith. Something with humor, to reflect his sparkling eyes and what went on behind them. She warmed to the thought that she knew him so well. It would be laborious, because every bit of digging would force her into thought about him. This, another exhausting thing, could be done in bits and pieces. There was no hurry. But it must be a cheerful, busy place, because although he wasn't always cheerful, he did try to be. And though he didn't always like how busy he was, he was busy. Good, she thought. He was busy because he didn't have as much time as others do. He had to fill a shorter amount of time with the important things he had to accomplish. She would fill the memorial garden with plants bulging everywhere. It would be slightly busy, over the top, unlike her own wavy, peaceful, meditative places. It would be another way to intertwine his memory with her own. Someday, when she could bear to think of him without absolutely piercing pain, she would plant in three seasons. One season missing: just like him. But beautiful. Just like him.

Memorial gardens are everywhere. Many cemeteries are called memorial gardens, but it's usually a stretch of the word. The things planted there are usually people, not plants. But find a gardener, and you will often find a memorial garden. Sometimes they are in memory of a friend who lost a battle with cancer. Sometimes they remember a parent, or a grandparent, or a child. There are usually plaques of some sort, with sayings that represent something about that loved one. Maybe there are windchimes, and usually, they are well cared for. There may be plants from the loved one's garden, and a symbol or two of their life. The gardens are for the living one to heal in, but they are all about never, ever forgetting the one to whom they are dedicated. Some are filled with rocks and paths, and some with swaying grasses and benches for meditation. They are important, and they are watered with many tears. They are beloved places with many secrets and stories.

There are types of healing gardens other than memorial gardens. Especially wonderful are gardens designed specifically for those with disabilities. More and more nursing homes have gardens where residents can sometimes share in the planting and weeding of favorite flowers and foods, and sometimes share in remembering their own garden wisdom to pass along. Garden beds can be raised high off the ground for those who are wheelchair-bound, and special tools with long handles can be acquired to help the disabled gardener reach the earth and imitate the Creator with their own creative capabilities. Breathing the fresh air outdoors and moving to the fullest extent possible, the disabled gardener can see the results of their own labor if a garden is designed with their abilities in mind.

For the blind, gardens full of scent are especially inviting. For those with mental disabilities, the soothing repetition makes garden tasks achievable, and the mentally disabled can acquire self-satisfaction from usefulness, and joy and surprise at the beauty.

For the terminally ill, gardens represent all the cycles of life and death within the short span of seasons. They teach the lessons of living life in full bloom, and dying with hope. The very labor that goes into maintaining a garden is exhausting, and not always doable. But it is a place to bury anger and find resolution and courage.

Yet another sort of healing garden is found in gardens planted with medicinal plants. Literally, these healing gardens were at one time the only source for dealing with the ravages of disease, pain, bleeding, fevers, or bellyaches. Very often they appear in literature as the gardens of old crones, moving slowly with the help of a crooked staff among plants that were as often poison as healing. In truth, early on they were even more often under the oversight of a religious order of some sort. In Europe, this was often the bailiwick of the area monastery. Within the monastery, a monk schooled in both the healing arts and horticulture superintended the healing garden. The most famous of these monks is Gerard, who wrote one of the first books on herbal healing, *Gerard's Herbal.*

In the lovely dimension of historical fiction, an even more familiar monk with a cloudy past found healing for his own soul as well as the maladies of others in the dimension of his own domain: the healing garden in the monastery at Shrewsbury. The monk's name was Brother Cadfael. The creation of writer Edith Parteger, who wrote under the pen name of Ellis Peters, Cadfael's rare mix of crime solving, understanding of sin because of his own spotted background, and identification with the humble and lowly make him winsome and lovable, as well as shrewd.

Brother Cadfael's adventures took place early in the twelfth century, mostly in rural southern England. A native of Wales himself, Cadfael's past as an accomplished and valiant knight with a rogue streak has been laid to rest in favor of a life dedicated to the service of the Lord. Posted in out-of-the-way Shrewsbury, Brother Cadfael's past life in war and worldliness serve him well in crime solving. He would much rather spend his days in his garden, discovering new ways to heal the diseases and ease the pains rife in the dark ages. His knowledge of horticulture helps him solve many of his crimes, as do his less admirable past experiences. Parteger uses Cadfael's character to illustrate one of her prevalent themes: God uses everything in lives devoted to Him—both that in which we take human pride and that which we would rather forget and even hide—for good.

A brilliant illustration of Romans 8:28, the fallible Cadfael speaks with simplicity to the sinners who read his adventures. He is sixty when he gives over to the life of a monk. The account of this sudden turning shows just why he was particularly ready for life in the garden:

"It was fair, he considered; it was enough. He turned and went away without another word. He went, just as he was, to Vespers in the parish church, for no better reason—or so he thought then—than that the dimness within the open doorway beckoned him as he turned his back on a duty completed, inviting him to quietness and thought, and the bell was just sounding. The little prior was there, ardent in thanksgiving, one more creature who had fumbled his way to the completion of a task, and the turning of a leaf in the book of his life.

"Cadfael watched out the office, and stood mute and still for some time after priest and worshippers had departed. The silence after their going was deeper than the ocean and more secure than the earth. Cadfael breathed and consumed it like new bread. It was the light touch of a small hand on the hilt of his sword that startled him out of that profound isolation. He looked down to see a little acolyte, no higher than his elbow, regarding him gravely from great round eyes of blinding blue, intent and challenging, as solemn as ever was angelic messenger.

"'Sir,' said the child in stern treble reproof, tapping the hilt with an infant finger, 'should not all weapons of war be laid aside here?'

"'Sir,' said Cadfael hardly less gravely, though he was smiling, 'you may very well be right.' And slowly he unbuckled the sword from his belt, and went and laid it down, flatlings, on the lowest step under the altar. It looked strangely appropriate and at peace there. The hilt, after all, was a cross."

A PRACTICUM ON WEEDING

We gardeners can get carried away. Gardening is awe-inspiring, and there are so many profound lessons to be learned. Like giving birth— or in a lesser sense painting, writing, or composing a piece of music— when we garden, we imitate God's creativity. We understand a little of the joy He felt at creation, and because we are made in His image, exercising this creative facet of our personalities brings pleasure.

Because our gardens bring us such serenity, because they are places we have designed ourselves in specific ways to mirror our own tastes, we feel good when we are in them. When we feel grumpy, we can go and weed awhile, and we feel better. Things look better afterward. While we weeded, we had the choice either to sort out the offending circumstances that drove us out there in the first place, or see it as a welcome distraction to think about nothing but tearing ugly things out, leaving room for good and beautiful things, and restoring order over one little area in our lives where we had some control.

When we are sad, we go to the garden for solace. At first, we just take in scents, then as we are stronger, we begin to pluck at things again. We pull a weed, deadhead a bud, and all those lessons we learned about life and death, beauty and plants past flowering, all the lessons we've ever learned about seasons and renewal come flooding back with force. We don't want winter to come for our loved ones, but it does, as surely as orderly seasons come each and every year—always have, and always will. And when sickness or death comes in spring, or summer, or fall, we know it's not right, because there was no fullness of seasons. Some plants are just weaker from the beginning. And we remember that every seed doesn't sprout, and some sprout early and die from frost, and on and on go the lessons until we realize we have stopped completely. We are staring at a place in the dirt where something used to be, we cry hot tears, and we feel sorrowful, but better somehow. We are part of the larger picture. We understand.

Or someone causes us great pain, and we march out to the garden. We put on our big, floppy hat and our sensible shoes, yank our gloves on, and put on the tank top that shows our aging arms. We march out to the garden shed and grab our bag of tools, huff out to the bed, and pull up that old plant we've watered, loved on, babied, cut back, trained up, and it still won't grow or bud, and it's ugly there, anyway. We just pull it out and are done with it. Why didn't we do it sooner? We look for things to cut back. We dig up that blackberry vine and replant it within bounds. We stomp around and shake the dirt out of our shoes, sweat and drink from the hose, and work until dark. There may even be dirt smeared on our face from hot tears that turned to mud when we tried to wipe them away. The garden looks more orderly when we go inside that night.

Important things happen in the garden. This is why our

thoughts can go so awry. Our little bed, or plot, or spot can become so symbolic of all we've felt there that we actually begin to think it's a magical place. Garden writing is full of symbols carried too far, images that become personified. That breeze in your sister's memorial garden, the one that stirs the wind chimes just as it also raises the scent of her favorite roses; it's just a breeze. Our wishes, our memories, and our sorrows are what infuse the breeze with thoughts that her spirit is there. There's a difference in allowing memory to be stirred and allowing our thoughts to take us places they really shouldn't go.

Fantasy, dreaminess, and flights of fancy are all useful in creativity and comfort, but even they must at some level be tempered with truth. Here is the choice: Will truth be viewed as a boundary to all freedom, or as the safe green pasture into which I have been shepherded? (Psalm 23)

So I choose carefully my garden ornamentation. I like beautiful things, symbolic things, musical things, and things that play with the light values across the growing things in my little patch of dirt. But I don't believe spirits inhabit the elements, or that angels lurk in the rosemary, or that certain herbs or configurations of plants will bring good or bad fortune. They will grow better in certain configurations. They will be healthier, happier plants (personification intended) when planted at certain times and in certain configurations, but that is not magic. That's just good gardening sense, kind of like common sense tells me which nights to wait up for my teenagers and which nights it's okay to go on to sleep before they come in.

It's good to remember that the gardener is learning from the orderly world already created; the gardener would do well to stay within this created order. Going outside the created order is called fiction, and as long as that is kept in mind, we're still in the pasture. But when we attempt to turn fiction into reality, we end up thinking the rabbit that ran past is a sign, or that the mockingbird is trying to communicate with us, or that the created can ever understand all the mysteries of the Creator.

Sometimes we have to weed our thought life.

The Vicarage Garden

Since the beginning of time, gardens have been associated with faith. It was in the Garden set at the center of the land of Eden where God first met with and communed with man. In every culture ever since, there has been something of the sacred attached to gardens. Not surprisingly then, churches and monasteries have often prominently featured gardens. And the homes of pastors have often been associated with gardens representing the solace of the entire covenant community. These vicarage gardens, as the English call them, are among the most beautiful and serene examples of the gardener's art in all the world.

Behind the wall of St. John's in the city,
In the shade of the garden, the Rector's wife
Walks with her baby, a girl, and the first,
Such a sight of life, of newness, of hope;
And all rightly situated: in the garden.
> ✥ TALBOT MATTHEWS (1884–1951) ✥

My garden, that skirted the avenue of the Manse, was of precisely
the right extent. An hour or two of morning labor was all that it
required. But I used to visit and revisit it a dozen times a day, and
stand in deep contemplation over my vegetable progeny with a love
that nobody could share or conceive of, who had never taken part in
the process of creation.
> ✥ NATHANIEL HAWTHORNE (1804–1864) ✥

I have caught hold of the earth—a marvelous gardener's phrase—and
neither my friends nor my enemies will find it an easy matter to
transplant me again.
> ✥ LORD BOLINGBROKE (1678–1751) ✥

There is no place more apt for a garden than upon the vicarage lawn or within the church yard. For what may better portray the Gospel than a garden, but with its tares and wheat growing up together until the day of harvest, but with its seeds dying and resurrecting, but with its promise of seasons, but with its fragrances of life and decay, but with its miraculous revelation of all that is good and right and true?

                     ❦ TRISTAN GYLBERD (1954–) ❧

'Twas in the vicarage garden where
I saw my soul unfold;
'Twas there delight and wisdom met
And solace from of old.

               ❦ JAMES CAMERON MCCRIE (1882–1971) ❧

The most important thing in a parish garden is not the garden itself, but rather, the setting it affords. It ought not be ostentation so as to overwhelm the people who walk in it, converse in it, pray in it, do business with God in it.

ZELDA FITZWILLIAM (1899–1942)

The church ought to be a garden sanctuary in the midst of the community. Thus, the vicarage garden is a kind of double symbolism of the mission of the Gospel in the world.

THOMAS GUIDRY (1779–1854)

If the church garden is a place of beauty, it will likely invoke a beauty in relationships and people's lives such that they become beautiful individually just as they are already beautiful corporately.

ALEXANDER BROWN (1801–1882)

In the quiet after Evensong
We took a turn in the garden,
There were no sounds whatever
Save the dripping of water from lilies
And the crickets in the clover.

In the quiet after Evensong
The garden stilled my storms
It calmed my greatest passions
And settled my gravest fears
Whilst soothing eyes in beauty.

In the quite after Evensong
I found my faith again
Not in sanctuary or dogma
But in the quiet voice
Which spoke so loud in flowers.

ஃ NEVILLE THEMSIC (1909–1988) ஃ

The church, the vicarage, and the garden are the hubs of any true community.

ISAAC GRANT (1883–1968)

A country parson without some knowledge of plants is surely as incomplete as a country parsonage without a garden.

JOSEPH WELLINGTON HUNKIN, C. 1988

Get a man into the fresh air,
Interest him in the marvelous works of God,
Instead of the deformities of vice,
Give him an occupation
Which will add to his health
And the comforts of his family,
Instead of destroying both,
Then build revealed upon natural revelation
And hope to see him a Christian.

DEAN SAMUEL REYNOLDS HOLE (1811–1899)

I suppose that the phrase *English Vicarage Garden* evokes for most of us a vision of striped lawns, herbaceous borders and ancient cedar trees, all bathed in the gentle sunshine of a summer's afternoon. It is understandable. When I was young, most vicarage gardens had a gardener to augment the incumbent's efforts, and church gardens were well-kept even when the vicar was not himself a gardener. The general public, whether churchgoers or not, were invited into these pleasances on specified summer afternoons to enjoy all the fun of the fair, bowling for the pig, riding on a miniature railway, home-made teas in a tent, and innumerable stalls, to raise funds for the church roof, the organ, or any of those ecclesiastical casualties which, like the poor, are always with us.

◦⊦ Miss Read, c. 1988 ⊹◦

The parish garden plot, where the pastor and his elders generally walked together for times of deep theological reflections, where the counselor and his parishioners met for instruction in the ways of wisdom, where the tutor gathered together his disciples for proper catechizing, where the intercessor found words for his heavenly supplications, and where the husbandman took hold of his familial duties, was the most used, most essential, and most spiritually inclined place of all. No wonder then that many presbyteries take more care with the planning and maintenance of the parish garden than the manse or even the meeting house. For, it was in the garden where the Lord's business was done.

❦ JOHN BUCHAN (1875–1940) ❧

Once a pastor has found out the advantages of proffering counsel in the garden, he will never again return to the stuffiness of an office or meeting room. For there in the garden will the reinforcements of God's truth in nature be afforded.

❦ CHARLES HIGGINS (1828–1894) ❧

One touch of nature makes the whole world kin.

❦ WILLIAM SHAKESPEARE (C. 1564–1616) ❧

Like two cathedral towers these stately pines
Uplift their fretted summits tipped with cones;
The arch beneath them is not built with stones,
Not art but nature traced these lovely lines,
And carved this graceful arabesque of vines;
No organ but the wind here sighs and moans,
No sepulcher conceals a martyr's bones,
No marble bishop on his tomb reclines.
Enter! The pavement carpeted with leaves,
Gives back a softened echo to my tread.
Listen! The choir is singing; all the birds,
In leafy galleries beneath the eaves,
Are singing! Listen, ere the sound be fled,
And learn there may be worship without words.

        ❁ HENRY WADSWORTH LONGFELLOW (1807–1882) ❁

Somehow, clergymen and their gardens go together in the layman's
view, probably because in days gone by the garden, like the church
and the vicarage itself, exerted a strong influence on the pattern of a
clergyman's life.

        ❁ MISS READ, C. 1988 ❁

St. Mary's Parish

Adjacent to Lambeth Palace just across the Thames from
Westminster is one of London's most delightful gardens. There,
within the tiny churchyard of St. Mary's Parish, is a carefully tended
walled plot bursting with color and fragrance.

A narrow brick-lined pathway winds through lush beds of for-
get-me-nots, polyanthus, and crown imperial fritillaries. What
appear to be haphazard clumps of lilac, viburnum, and philadel-
phus are linked integrally to one another by a wide wavy border
planted with alchemilla, nepeta, and several other sturdy herbaceous plants that I've never quite been able to identify. There are
assorted blooming primroses, lilies, and canterbury bells in spring
and snapdragons, hardy geraniums, and lavender in summer. Along
one wall, in front of a magnificent wisteria, is a bed redolent with
herbs—basil, thyme, oregano, and cilantro. There is parsley among
the hollyhocks, honeysuckle twisted round the roses, and tiger
lilies peaking through the shrubby euphorbias. It is a hard-won
taste of paradise planted in the midst of a hustle-bustle urban
sprawl.

Though the celebrated English gardens of Hever Castle, of
Sissinghurst, or of Glyndebourne are certainly more spectacular, it is
this little parish vicar's garden that epitomizes for us all what a garden ought to be. Its personal scale, its wide-ranging palette, and its

orderly conception portray a distinctly practical vision of both the possibilities and the limitations of this poor fallen world.

As if to underscore this truth, a little bronze plaque adorning one corner of the garden declares: "A good theology will invariably produce a good garden." The first time we read that we chuckled and quickly dismissed it as just another bit of gardener's hyperbole. But then, the more we thought about it the more we began to realize that the plaque's epigram actually conveys a uniquely scriptural worldview.

A good theology is more than the sum of its parts. While it is composed of certain essential dogmas and doctrines, each of those essentials must also be carefully related to all the others. It sees all too clearly the crucial connection between the profound and the mundane. While it wisely attends to the minutest of details, it also remains fully cognizant of how those details affect the bigger picture. It places as much significance on the bits and pieces as it does on the totals.

A good theology is good for the soul. But it is also good for the world. Its spiritual vision gives vitality to all that it touches—from flower gardens and herbiaries to nation-states and cultures—simply because the integrity of that vision ultimately depends as much on a balanced biblical worldview as on a solid scriptural soteriology. Its attention to heavenly concerns is integrally bound to its fulfillment of earthly responsibilities.

Of course, actually making that connection between heavenly concerns and earthly responsibilities is never easy. We are all constantly tugged between piety and practicality, between devotion and duty, between communion with God and calling in the world. Like tending a well-groomed garden, honing a balanced biblical worldview involves both the drudgery of daily labor and the high ideals of faith, hope, and love. But the results are always worth the extra effort.

The little vicarage garden of St. Mary's served a rural parish until well into the Victorian age, when the London sprawl swallowed it up. It was a gathering place for church functions. It served as an extra office for the pastors of the parish to conduct counseling sessions, to hold meetings, to study and read, to pray, and to think. Through the years, it remained intimately scaled, carefully planned, lovingly tended, and heavily used.

Vicarage gardens have always been an important feature of British life. It was always a kind of integration point for the larger community, an informal gathering place, an unofficial alternation to the sanctuary or the town hall where the covenant bonds of a life lived together might be strengthened and renewed.

Like hundreds of other little vicarage gardens all around the British Isles, the plot of St. Mary's parish is hardly the sort of spectacular demonstration of horticultural prowess that some botanical gardens can boast. Nor does it bear the marks of a single genius.

Instead, it portrays that unique and quiet virtue of ordinariness and community. It revels in that old principle of the Gospel that proclaims that we may find the heroic in the mundane, not in the profane; we may find glory in commonness, not in prominence.

Not surprisingly, the British Garden Society chose this little garden to be the site of its national gardening museum in 1987. Today, St. Mary's continues to wield an influence all out of proportion to its size and importance. Like all good vicarage gardens its whole was greater than the sum of its parts.

A good theology—with its comprehensive worldview—inevitably affects the world for good. A bad theology—with its fragmented worldview—sows only tares. That is an important truth that the vicarage garden of St. Mary's parish taught us.

A Practicum on Theology

The Christian view of the world and all the things of the world is fraught with a sort of gardener's paradox—an appreciation for both the potentialities and the liabilities of fallen creation. It is a worldview that is actually reinforced and enlightened by the simple tasks of gardening.

We know for instance, that the world is only a temporary dwelling place. It is "passing away" (1 John 2:17), and we are here but for a little while as "strangers and sojourners" (Leviticus 25:23).

Because we are a part of "the household of God" (Ephesians 2:19), our true "citizenship is in heaven" (Philippians 3:20). Our affections are naturally set on "things above" (Colossians 3:2).

In addition, the world is filled with dangers, toils, and snares (Jeremiah 18:22). In tandem with "the flesh and the devil," it makes "war with the saints" (Revelation 13:7). "All that is in the world—the lust of the flesh, the lust of the eyes, and the pride of life—is not of the Father but is of the world" (1 John 2:16). The world cannot receive "the Spirit of truth" (John 14:17) because "the cares of this world . . . choke the word," and it becomes unfruitful (Matthew 13:22).

Thankfully, Christ overcame the world (John 16:33) and then chose us out of the world (John 15:19). Thus, we are not to be "conformed to this world" (Romans 12:2), neither are we to "love the world" (1 John 2:15) because Christ "gave Himself for our sins, that He might deliver us from this present evil age" (Galatians 1:4). Though we once "walked according to the course of this world" (Ephesians 2:2), now we are to keep ourselves "unspotted from the world" (James 1:27). Indeed, "friendship with the world is enmity with God" so that whoever is "a friend of the world makes himself an enemy of God" (James 4:4).

Thus, warnings against worldliness, carnal mindedness, and earthly attachments dominate biblical ethics. As Oswald Chambers has said: "The counsel of the Spirit of God to the Saints is that they must allow nothing worldly in themselves while living among the worldly in the world."

But then, that is the problem, isn't it? We must continue to live in the world. We must be "in" it but not be "of" it. And that is no easy feat. As John Calvin wrote in his helpful little *Golden Booklet of the True Christian Life*: "Nothing is more difficult than to forsake all carnal thoughts, to subdue and renounce our false appetites, and to devote ourselves to God and our brethren, and to live the life of angels in a world of corruption."

And to make matters even more complex, we not only have to live in this dangerous fallen world, but we have to work in it (1 Thessalonians 4:11), serve in it (Luke 22:26), and minister in it (2 Timothy 4:5). We have been appointed ambassadors to it (2 Corinthians 5:20), priests for it (1 Peter 2:9), and witnesses in it (Matthew 24:14). We even have to go to "the end of the earth" (Acts 1:8), offering a "good confession" of the eternal life to which we were called (1 Timothy 6:12).

The reason for this seemingly contradictory state of affairs— enmity with the world on the one hand, responsibility to it on the other—is simply that "God so loved the world that He gave His only begotten Son" (John 3:16). Though the world is "under the sway of the wicked one" (1 John 5:19) and knows not God, (1 Corinthians 1:21), God is "in Christ reconciling the world to Himself" (2 Corinthians 5:19). Jesus is "the light of the world" (John

8:12). He is the "Savior of the world" (1 John 4:14). He is the "Lamb of God who takes away the sin of the world" (John 1:29). Indeed, He was made "the propitiation for our sins, and not for ours only but also for the whole world" (1 John 2:2). Through Christ all things are reconciled to the Father (Colossians 1:20) so that finally "the kingdoms of this world have become the kingdoms of our Lord and of His Christ" (Revelation 11:15).

A genuinely integrated Christian worldview must be cognizant of both perspectives of the world—and treat them with equal weight. It must be engaged in the world. It must be unengaged in worldliness. It must somehow correlate spiritual concerns with temporal concerns. It must coalesce heavenly hope and landed life. It must coordinate heartfelt faith and down-to-earth practice.

In other words, it is a whole lot like gardening—and thus, is essentially and integrally compatible with it. This is one of the reasons why—all practical pastoral care aside—so much good theology through the years has utilized garden imagery, relied on garden themes, and been written in garden environs (one has only to think of such works as Augustine's *Confessions*, Calvin's *Institutes*, and Kuyper's *Pro Rege*). It is, after all, difficult to take theology too terribly far east of Eden.

The Artist's Garden

The longing for home is woven into the fabric of the life of every man, every woman, and every child. It is profoundly affected by their inescapable connection to places, persons, and principles—the incremental parts of a covenant community. While the nomad spirit of modernity has dashed the integrity of community, it has done nothing to alter the need for it. Gardens serve to connect us with those places, persons, and principles in remarkable and unexpected ways. This is a notion that wise men and women through the ages—and particularly wise artists, musicians, and writers—seem to have always known. It is part of that spark of genius that makes their work live on long after they themselves have passed on into eternity.

I believe it is no wrong observation, that persons of genius, and those most capable of art, are always most fond of nature, as such are chiefly sensible, that all art consists in the imitation and study of nature.

❧ ALEXANDER POPE (1688–1774) ☙

When I go into my garden with a spade, and dig a bed, I feel such an exhilaration and health that I discover that I have been defrauding myself all this time in letting others do for me what I should have done with my own hands.

❧ RALPH WALDO EMERSON (1803–1882) ☙

I hope you will survey a low sea of gray clumps of foliage, pierced here and there with tall white flowers. I visualize the white trumpets of dozens of Regale lilies, grown three years ago from seed, coming up through the gray of southernwood and artemesia and cotton-lavender, with gray-and-white edging plants such as Dianthus Mrs. Sinkins and the silvery mats of Stachys lanata, more familiar and so much nicer under its English name of Rabbit's Ears or Savior's Flannel. There will be white pansies, and white peonies, and white irises with their gray leaves, at least, I hope there will be all these things. All the same, I cannot help hoping that the gray barn-owl will sweep silently across a pale garden, next summer in the twi-light—the pale garden that I am now planting, under the first flakes of snow.

           VITA SACKVILLE-WEST (1892–1962)

To be happy at home is the end of all labor.

           SAMUEL JOHNSON (1709–1784)

Every man, though he were born
In the very belfry of Bow
And spent his infancy climbing among the chimneys,
He has waiting for him somewhere a country house
Which he has never seen,
But which was built for him
In the shape of his soul.
It stands patiently waiting to be found;
And when the man sees it he remembers it,
Though he has never seen it before.
                    ◦[G. K. CHESTERTON (1874–1936)]◦

It is impossible for any culture to be sound and healthy without a
proper respect and proper regard for the soil.
                    ◦[ANDREW NELSON LYTLE (1902–1995)]◦

One of the strangest disparities of history lies between the sense of
abundance felt by older and simpler societies and the sense of
scarcity felt by the ostensibly richer societies of today. Perhaps the
difference is the loss of community that so afflicts us today—in stark
contrast to those happier cultures of days gone by.
                    ◦[RICHARD WEAVER (1910–1963)]◦

Hearth and home are the cornerstones of help and hope and happiness.

– MARK TWAIN (1835–1910) –

I know a beautiful lovely garden. There are many children in it picking up apples under the trees, and pears, cherries, and plums; they sing, hop about and are happy. I asked a man whose garden it was whose children they were. He answered: they are the children that like to pray and learn and are pious—as would be the case in any garden in this world, of course.

– MARTIN LUTHER (1483–1546) –

Do not bemoan the turn of fortune that makes of a simple matter a heroic act.

– ANDREW NELSON LYTLE (1902–1995) –

After the war, says the papers, they'll no be content at hame,
The lads hae feucht wi' death twae 'ear I' the mud
And the rain and the snaw; for aifter a sadger's life
The shop will be unco tame; they'll ettle at fortune and freedom
In the new lands far awa.
No me. By God. No me.
Aince we hae lickit oor faes and aince I get oot o' this hell,
For the rest o' my leevin' days I'll mak a pet o' mysel.
I'll haste meback wi' an eident fit and settle again in the same auld
bit.
And oh, the comfort to snowkagain the reek o' my mither's but-and-
ben,
The wee box-bed and the ingle neuk, and the kail-pat hung frae the
chimley-hook.
I'll gang back to the shop like a laddie to play,
Tak doun the shutters at skreigh o' day,
And weigh oot floor wi' a carefu' pride, and hear the clash o' the
countraside.

✤ JOHN BUCHAN (1875–1940) ✤

Any woodsman can tell you that in a broken and sundered nest, one can hardly expect to find more than a precious few whole eggs. So it is with the family.

⊹ THOMAS JEFFERSON (1743–1826) ⊱

The woods that once overhung the reaches of the river behind his boyhood home came back to him so clearly that for the sake of them, and to enjoy their beauty, he put his hand in front of his eyes, and he saw with every delicate appeal that one's own woods can offer, the steep bank beyond the barn, the high ridge which hid the view from the town, and the rapids which turned and hurried below. He smelt the fresh mown hay. Not ever, in a better time, when he had seen it of reality and before his own eyes living, had that good picture been so plain; and even the colors of it were more vivid than they commonly are in the Southern air; but because it was a vision there was hardly a sound, he couldn't even hear the rustling of the leaves, though he was able to make out the whistling of the breeze gusty on the water-meadow banks, and the ruffling force against the stream. For a moment, soft out of the night, he even thought he heard his father quoting Homer—as he had so often done with an answering heart—that "he longed as he journeyed to see once more the smoke going up from his own land, and after that to die."

⊹ TRISTAN GYLBERD (1954–) ⊱

Midway this way of life we're bound upon,
I woke to find myself in a dark wood,
Where the right road was wholly lost and gone.

Ay me! How hard to speak of it—that rude
And rough and stubborn forest! The mere breath
Of memory stirs the old fear in the blood;

It is so bitter, it goes nigh to death;
Yet there I gained such good, that, to convey
The tale, I'll write what else I found therewith.

How I got into it I cannot say,
Because I was so heavy and full of sleep
When first I stumbled from the narrow way.

❧ DANTE ALIGHIERI (1265–1321) ☙

There arose in me a multitude of thoughts
Through which at last came floating a vision
Of the woods of home and of another place;
The lake where the Arun rises.
And I said to myself, inside my own mind:
What are you doing?
You are on some business that takes you far,
Not even for ambition or for adventure,
But only to earn.
And you will cross the sea and earn your money,
And you will come back and spend more than you have earned.
But all the while your life runs past you like a river,
And the things that are of moment to men
You do not heed at all.

          ❧ HILAIRE BELLOC (1870–1953) ❧

The most extraordinary thing in the world is an ordinary man and an ordinary woman and their ordinary children.

⊰ G. K. CHESTERTON (1874–1936) ⊱

We were born on the same soil, breathe the same air, live on the same land, so why should we not be brothers and sisters?

⊰ NATHAN BEDFORD FORREST (1821–1877) ⊱

The community is the true sphere of human virtue. In social, active life, difficulties will perpetually be met with; restraints of many kinds will be necessary; and studying to behave right in respect of these, is a discipline of the human heart, useful to others, and improving to itself.

⊰ SAMUEL JOHNSON (1709–1784) ⊱

When, in disgrace with fortune and men's eyes,
I all alone beweep my outcast state,
And trouble deaf heaven with my bootless cries,
And look upon myself and curse my fate,
Wishing me like to one more rich in hope,
Featured like him, like him with friends possessed,
Desiring this man's art and that man's scope,
With what I most enjoy contented least:
Yet in these thoughts myself most despising,
Haply I think on thee, and then my state,
Like to the lark at break of day arising
From sullen earth, sings hymns at heaven's gate;
For thy sweet love remembered such wealth brings
That then I scorn to change my state with kings.

❧ WILLIAM SHAKESPEARE (C. 1564–1616) ❧

Attachment to the soil is an inescapable aspect of the healthy psyche. Uprootedness is a kind of psychosis—sadly, rampant in our community-less society.

❧ MARTIN LEMBEC (1909–1990) ❧

The sin of egotism always takes the form of withdrawal. When personal advantage becomes paramount, the individual passes out of the community.

❧ RICHARD WEAVER (1910–1963) ❧

Monet's Giverny

The son of a successful tradesman in marine supplies, Claude Monet grew up in Le Havre on the Normandy coast. He showed signs of artistic talent as a teenager, drawing skillful caricatures of local personalities. He would spend hours at a time along the shore, at the docks, and in his family's little seaside garden, sketching everything within sight. He would later confess that he never felt so alive as when he was in his "own little plot, imitating with pen and ink and rough sketch book."

That would be a theme that would mark his life and his affections ever afterward.

Over time, he came to admire the work of many of the more adventurous artists of his day, landscapists associated with the Barbizon School, such as Camille Corot, Charles-François Daubigny, Constant Troyon, and Henri Rousseau. The Barbizon painters promoted landscape painting that stood without reference to historic, religious, or mythological stories, a concept that was then new to French art.

Monet also admired French realist artists Gustave Courbet and Honoré Daumier. The realists depicted members of the working classes and their domestic environments, which until then had been considered unworthy subjects for art. Monet received crucial early guidance from two artists who specialized in painting seascapes out-of-doors, Eugène Boudin, a fellow painter from Le Havre, and Dutch artist Johan Barthold Jongkind, whom Monet met in 1862. The unusual viewpoints—scenes shown from above or below—and broad areas of bright color in Japanese woodblock prints also influenced Monet's work.

Monet's formal art training began in 1859 at the Académie Suisse, a studio that provided models for aspiring artists to draw or paint, but gave little direct instruction. Another future leader of the impressionist art world, Camille Pissarro, was a fellow student there, and the two soon became close friends, often meeting in the school's cloistered garden to talk, sketch, and dream.

After serving briefly in the French military in Algeria, Monet joined a Parisian studio run by Charles Gabriel Gleyre in 1862. Gleyre's studio was essentially student-run. Like the Académie Suisse, it encouraged students to draw from models, rather than from plaster casts of ancient Greek and Roman statues, which was the common teaching method of more conservative academies. In Gleyre's studio Monet met several artists who would become fellow impressionists, Auguste Renoir, Alfred Sisley, and Frédéric Bazille.

In 1865 Monet had his first works—two ambitious seascapes— accepted by the Salon, a juried art exhibition sponsored annually by the official French Academy of Fine Arts. Thereafter he had a checkered record of acceptance and rejection by the conservative Salon jury, although his works received praise from critics such as

French writer Émile Zola and were purchased by discerning and influential buyers.

It was then that Monet's work began to gravitate once again to natural and/or garden themes. His massive works *Luncheon on the Grass*, a picnic scene that measured fifteen feet by twenty feet, and *Women in the Garden*, which was almost that size, convinced the artist to collaborate with Renoir on a series of landscapes *en plein air* (outdoors) at a fashionable bathing place, La Grenouillère, on the Seine River near Paris. In these small works, Monet's quick daubs of fresh colors aptly captured the movement of the water and gaiety of the scene—and eventually gave birth to the impressionist movement.

The painters who became known as impressionists began exhibiting together in 1874. They held eight exhibitions between 1874 and 1886, and although Monet did not participate in all of these, he became the most celebrated member of the group, and remains so today.

Gardens were a recurrent theme for Monet, and paintings of his own garden dominated his later work. In 1890 he purchased a house in Giverny that he had been renting for seven years. He began to develop its gardens, introducing an ornamental lily pond and a Japanese-style bridge. These and other features of his idyllic estate were the subject of a steady output of large decorative paintings. He generally began by painting out in the garden itself, but would then return to his studio to work and rework his canvases, which had become even more layered and complex than before.

Monet was passionate about gardening—indeed, it became increasingly difficult for him to separate his vocation as a painter from his avocation as a gardener. At his estate in Giverny, he cultivated three separate spaces. His two-acre flower garden, the Clos Normand, extended from his house to a railway line (now a busy highway). The second was a two-acre walled vegetable garden, surrounded by espaliered fruit trees and located at the opposite end of the house toward the village, and the third was his water garden on the other side of the railroad tracks. One look at the gardens and it is evident that Monet was home here. Indeed, one look at the gardens and it is evident that the whole idea of home had subsumed every other concern and every other interest. Monet discovered what mattered most, and it integrated the personal, the public, the professional, and the private.

Today, visitors can see Monet's carefully wrought handiwork—both on canvas and upon the soil—from April through October. The garden and the museum, taken together, afford a rare glimpse into the intersecting worlds of art and domesticity, of calling and life.

A Practicum on Home

There is no place like home. Of joy, of peace, of plenty, where supporting and supported, dear souls mingle into the blissful hubbub of daily life. No matter how benevolent, no matter how philanthropic, and no matter how altruistic some social or cultural alternative may be, it can never hope to match the personal intimacy of domestic relations. Except in the rare and extreme cases where strife and bitterness have completely disintegrated familial identity, there is no replacement for the close ties of brothers and sisters, fathers and mothers, husbands and wives, parents and children, aunts and uncles, kith and kin. Though under siege in our day, domesticity has always been recognized as the glue that holds nations together—and ever it shall be.

During what a few unreconstructed Southerners sometimes call the Late Lamentable Unpleasantness—what nearly everyone else calls the Civil War—the Confederate government issued regulations listing the diseases that might afflict the Rebel troops and hinder them in battle. One of these was a problem peculiar to soldiers who hailed from middle Tennessee. It seems that among the debilitating and sometimes life-threatening diseases on that list was an affliction that the field physicians aptly called *nostalgia*, from the Greek word meaning "a yearning to return home."

The longing for home is woven into the fabric of the life of every man, every woman, and every child. It is profoundly affected by their inescapable connection to places, persons, and principles—the incremental parts of a covenant community. While the nomad spirit of modernity has dashed the integrity of community, it has done nothing to alter the need for it. Covenantal attachment has always been an inescapable aspect of the healthy psyche—and it always will be. Uprootedness has always been a kind of psychosis—likewise, it always will be. Hearth and home are the cornerstones of help, hope, and happiness.

Humanness cannot be found in escape, detachment, absence of commitment, and undefined freedom—instead its great promise may only be found in those rare places where people have established identity, defined vocation, and envisioned destiny. It comes from the sense of connection to land and people and heritage that occurs when people try to provide continuity and identity across generations. Such a commitment is inevitably costly—but that is precisely what makes home so infinitely priceless.

That kind of covenantal attachment to home cannot simply occur anywhere—it must be intentionally rooted somewhere specific, somewhere unique, somewhere preclusive, somewhere that is inherently good and right and true.

The foundations of a civilized moral order are contentment with domestic conciliation, reverence for our forefathers, and compliance with our prescriptive duties. In other words, the crux of social cohesion is necessarily the happy home. Home is the answer to virtually all the ills of the world—both the wider world of mayhem and woe and the inner world of mishap and worry.

Home is, after all, the basic building block of society. When the home begins to break down, the rest of society begins to disintegrate. There is no replacement for the home. The government can't substitute services for it. Social workers can't substitute kindness and understanding for it. Educators can't substitute knowledge, skills, or understanding for it.

There are any number of reasons for this. The home provides men, women, and children with a proper sense of identity. In the midst of their home, people can know and be known as nowhere else. They can taste the joys and sorrows of genuine intimacy. They can gain a vision of life that is sober and sure. They can be bolstered by its love. They can be strengthened by its confidence. They can be emboldened by its legacy. And they can be stabilized by its objectivity. Everyone desperately needs that kind of perspective. They desperately need to be stabilized in the gentle environs of hearth and home.

In addition, though, home life provides men with a genuine social security. There is no place like home. In times of trouble our greatest resource will always be those who know us best and love us most. Because family members share a common sense of destiny with one another and a bond of intimacy to one another, they can—and will—rush to one another's sides when needed. And well they should. The home is an incubator for sound values. It reinforces the principles of authority, structure, liability, obedience, and selflessness. The accountability and discipline of home bring out the very best in us. A typical mother or father, without thinking twice about it, would willingly die, in a fire or accident, say, in order to save one of his or her children. While in most circumstances this human act would be regarded as heroic, for parents it is only ordinary.

Men ought to go somewhere. But modern man, in his sick reaction, is ready to go anywhere—so long as it is the other end of nowhere. We may well loathe the impulse to modernity, and yet we all have become the quintessentially modern man. Thus, a person travels the world over in search of what he needs and returns home to find it—even if that home is a place he has never really seen before.